THE SECRET WAR

THE SECRET WAR

by Ben Dan

SABRA BOOKS NEW YORK

ISBN 0-87631-043-9
Library of Congress Catalog Card Number 76-134359
Printed in Israel
Copyright © Librairie Artheme Fayard
Translated from the French edition "Poker d'Espions" published
by Librairie Artheme Fayard, 1970 by Jacqueline Kahanoff,
edited by Robert Gamzey
English Rights Reserved by Sabra Books, New York

CONTENTS

INTRODUCTION

One day, in Saint Helena, Napoleon told the British governor of the island that, in his opinion, Egypt was the most important country in the world. But, the defeated Emperor added, in order to conquer and keep Egypt, it was necessary to become master of the whole Mediterranean.

Substitute the term "Middle East" for that of "Egypt," and Napoleon's sally could provide a concise definition of the political and military strategy of the U.S.S.R. in the region. This strategy has become very clear since the Six Day War when Israel defeated her Arab neighbors, but since June 1956 when Nasser nationalized the Suez Canal, Soviet policy had already taken its decisive step in this direction.

Since then, everything would seem to indicate that, in conformity with the strategic principle defined by Napoleon, the U.S.S.R. considers the Middle East as the most important part of the world.

First the U.S.S.R. gained a foothold in Egypt, Syria,

Iraq, the Yemen, in the Sudan, and then in Algeria. Then she consolidated her positions in this part of the world by providing massive economic aid and offensive weapons to the governments of those countries. Then she despatched to them her technicians, engineers and officers, particularly to Egypt, Syria and Algeria. Then the U.S.S.R. provoked the Six Day War. The Arab defeat, ironically, gave the Soviet Union a further opportunity to extend its already overwhelming influence in most countries of the region. Thus, the U.S.S.R. proceeded to establish naval bases in Syria (Latakich), in Egypt (Alexandria and Port Said), in Algeria, (Mers el Kebir), and the Soviet Navy established itself in the Mediterranean on a par with the U.S. Navy. Last but not least, in the spring of 1970, the whole world became aware of the aims of Russian strategy as Soviet pilots took over the aerial defense of Egyptian towns, and then installed Sam 3 missiles west of the Suez Canal.

The Soviet Union's interest in the Middle East is many-sided and assumes a variety of forms. Strategically the "Arab areas" extend over a length of six thousand kilometers, mostly along the Mediterranean coastline, from the Atlantic shore of Morocco to Iran on the Persian Gulf. From a geo-political point of view, this region is at the crossroads of Asia, Africa and Europe, with the Suez Canal linking the Mediterranean to the Indian Ocean through the Red Sea. It is worth recalling here that control of the Suez Canal twice insured Allied victory over Germany and its various allies. This region has been the springboard of a movement of national

*awakening and liberation which has swept through from
Cairo, Damascus and Algeria, to other developing countries of Asia and Africa.*

*The economic importance of the Middle East is ob-
vious, with its inexhaustible oil resources, a large part of
which are still unexploited. The black gold the U.S.S.R.
could obtain at low cost should these oil reserves be
nationalized by Arab governments, besides providing it
with the means of insuring a more rapid rate of growth
for the countries within the Soviet orbit would also, in
the long run, give the Soviet Union an effective lever
over Western Europe, still largely dependent on Arab oil.*

*Finally, the U.S.S.R. has a purely political interest
in the Middle East. The friendship and political support
of Arab countries with a population of over one hundred
million, and the growing number of Arab votes in international institutions constitute an undoubted political
asset. Another aspect of Soviet political interest in the
Middle East, which became clear after General de Gaulle
gave French policy a pronounced pro-Arab and anti-
Israel orientation, is that divisions and antagonisms have
appeared among the countries of the Western bloc. These
divisions within the Western bloc are direct consequences
of Soviet policy towards Arab countries.*

*Since 1955-56, the U.S.S.R. has supplied the Arab
world with sums amounting to about half of a budget
worth five billion dollars, ear marked for non-communist
countries. Furthermore, Arab countries received more
than one third of Soviet economic aid to non-communist
countries. Since 1952, Egypt alone received more than*

a billion dollars from the U.S.S.R. to which must be added six hundred million dollars offered by other communist bloc countries. During the same period, the Western bloc headed by the United States provided about 1.8 billion dollars worth of aid. Since June 1967, the Egyptian Army, practically destroyed by Israel, has been reconstructed with the help of the Soviet Union and its allies. U.S.S.R. investments in Egypt in the course of a few years amounted to between two to four billion dollars. Such figures underline the scope of Soviet involvement in the Middle East. The presence of some sixty units of the Soviet fleet in the Mediterranean, once an exclusive Anglo-American preserve, gives additional emphasis to the Soviet presence in the area.

This strategy, obviously, is backed by a corresponding level of activities of Soviet Intelligence Services. These activities, operating through a variety of ways, from "passive" intelligence, through subversion, to active intervention in the internal affairs of the States in the region, preceded and secretly prepared the ground for official political and military decisions. The most striking example of the Soviet Union's secret activity in the Middle East, directly involves its responsibility in the sequence of events leading to the outbreak of the Six Day War, a responsibility which the U.S.S.R., using every means at its disposal, is attempting to shift on to Israel in the first place and, in second place to the United States.

On May 13, 1967 President Nasser received a message from Soviet Intelligence, conveyed through the Soviet Ambassador in Cairo, to the effect that the Soviet

Union had "precise information"* concerning the imminence of an Israeli attack against Syria.

Moscow even specified when Israeli troops would
attack Syria early on May 17. This "precise information"
was very much in line with that published by the Soviet
press — particularly Pravda, Trud, Izvestia and Kraznaja
Sverdie — which since October 1966 had periodically
announced the imminence of an Israeli attack against
Syria.

But in 1967, Soviet secret services really surpassed
themselves in bringing matters to a boiling point. Having
informed Nasser of an imminent Israeli attack, they also
provided him with "a precise survey" of Israeli troop
concentrations near the Syrian border, and even with
blueprints of the attack. The Syrian General Staff received the same information, from the same source, but
transmitted this time through a special Moscow envoy.
Damascus immediately informed Cairo, where the information was, of course, "old hat."

A fatal mechanism was thus set off, which precipitated the war and brought about the defeat of the Arab
armies.

On May 14, the U.A.R. mobilized its forces. That
same day, the first Egyptian divisions took up their positions in Sinai, along the Israeli border. On May 15,
Mohamed Fawzi, the Egyptian Chief-of-Staff met in Damascus with Syria's military chiefs; on May 16, Egypt

---

* Nasser himself referred to this message in his "resignation"
speech of June 9, 1967.

declared a state of emergency and continued to pour troops into Sinai; they were to number more than one hundred thousand within a week. Israel tried in vain to establish its good faith and invited the U.S.S.R. Ambassador in Tel Aviv to visit the Syrian border and see for himself that there were no troop concentrations. But the Ambassador, politely declining the invitation, repeated — in accordance with instructions received from his Government — the Kremlin's warnings concerning "Israel's projected attack against Syria."

Then came the withdrawal of U.N. troops from Gaza and Sharm el Sheik, Nasser's blockade of the Gulf of Akaba on May 23, Israel's qualms, the series of consultations of its representatives with Western world leaders in Paris, London and, first and foremost in Washington and finally, its lightning attack against Egypt on the morning of June 5.

Within six days, the game was over.

Since June 11, 1967, Israel controls the Straits of Tiran, whose closure by Nasser precipitated the War, all of Sinai to the Suez Canal, Transjordan, the Gaza strip and the Golan Heights, as well as Jerusalem, united under Israel's sovereign rule.

Did Soviet intelligence miscalculate when it informed Cairo and Damascus of an alleged Israeli attack against Syria? True enough, in the past, its services were often off the mark in evaluating the intentions of foreign powers, even in countries where the U.S.S.R. had access to a good deal of information in the enemy camp. Thus, Soviet intelligence predicted neither the invasion of the

Introduction

Soviet Union by Hitler's division, nor the firm resolve of Western powers to break the blockade of Berlin in 1948. In Korea, in 1950, then in Cuba, in 1962, these services committed serious errors. Yet, in 1967, it is highly improbable that Moscow believed for a single moment that Israel had any intention of invading Syria. The fact that the U.S.S.R. Ambassador to Israel refused to check on the situation prevailing along the Israeli-Syrian border — and recalling the Soviet press campaign concerning Israel's alleged war preparations against Syria — indicates that the U.S.S.R. deliberately planned to create a state of extreme tension in the Middle East. Still worse, one is entitled to believe that having provoked the crisis of May 13, the U.S.S.R. resolutely pushed the Arab States to war. It is generally thought that Nasser decided to close the Straits of Tiran without informing Moscow. That is possible. But Moscow was certainly aware that Israel, for whom the Straits represent a vital interest, would sooner or later have to take the initiative — yet did nothing to de-escalate the crisis on the Arab side. Quite the opposite. Moscow promised its support to the Arabs, while abstaining from pledging its direct military intervention. Moscow thus cold-headedly played the card of an Israeli Arab War, knowing full well that the Soviet Union stood to win in any event, whatever the outcome of the war. Victorious, the Arabs would have been grateful to the U.S.S.R. for having encouraged them to make war on Israel, and having supplied them with military and technical assistance. Defeated, they would have no other choice but to turn to Moscow to obtain

13

the necessary support in the international arena to press for Israel's withdrawal, and the military, technical and financial support to rebuild their shattered forces. Thus, the U.S.S.R. did nothing to dissociate itself from Nasser's stand of May 23, which meant war, just as the U.S.S.R. did nothing to prevent the Arab defeat from being a total one. Furthermore, the U.S.S.R. had long known that Israeli pilots flying French Mirages were superior to Arab pilots flying Soviet Migs. It also knew that Israel's armored divisions would crush Egyptian armor in Sinai. The U.S.S.R. thus cynically placed its bets on a war that would inevitably lead the Arabs to their defeat, thereby increasing their dependence on Moscow. This defeat gave the Soviet Union its chance to tighten its hold on Egypt and Syria, to assign to those countries, thousands of technicians and officers, including pilots, and to introduce the Sam 3 missiles.

These two countries have become Russian bases. The Arab defeat also gave the Soviet Union the opportunity to station many bomber squadrons in Algeria, and to bring the Soviet fleet into the Mediterranean.

Moscow's calculations have been exactly revealed. The Soviet position in the Middle East and the Mediterranean has been considerably strengthened since 1967, even more so since 1970. Nasser owed his political survival exclusively to Moscow, and he knew it. The Syrian Ba'ath party remains in power solely because of the police regime. The Arabs were defeated, but Israel finally won only a local victory, which has allowed it to survive and prepare either for peace, or for the next war against the Arabs. But Moscow has won, thanks to the defeat of its protegés, a strategic battle on a world-wide scale. In the future, whether for peace or war, the fate of the Middle East depends on the Soviet Union quite as much as on the United States.

The story of Israel Beer, the Soviet spy in Israel, which is told in the following pages, shows that the Soviet will to penetrate into the Middle East goes back to the 1920's. This story throws into bold relief the methods used by the Soviet Union to plant a secret agent in the highest political and military spheres of a country it regards as a key to this part of the world.

THE AUTHORS

PART I

SOVIET ESPIONAGE

CHAPTER ONE

THE CASE OF BEER

It was the first night of Passover, March 28, 1961, and commercial life, transportation, industry, entertainment, and normal daily activity had ground to a halt for the holiday of Jewish freedom. Only an isolated cafe remained open in scattered neighborhoods, offering a dismal haven for the friendless who had no Seder of their own, or invitation to the joyous gatherings of families and friends around the candle-lit, heavily laden tables, with the traditional wine and matzos.

"For the Lord thy God doth bring thee unto a good land, a land with streams of water, springs and deeps coming forth into the valley and the mountain, a land of wheat and barley and vines and fig trees and pomegranates, a land of olive oil and honey, a land wherein thou shalt not eat bread scantily."

And it was so, for the people of Israel reborn had made their stony hills and malarial valleys blossom and they were eating of the produce of their labors in this festival of their freedom.

"Avadim hayinu, ata bnei horin." "Slaves were we,

19

and now we are free men." The Passover Haggadah spoke of prayers fulfilled and dreams come true. Israel was free again in its own land.

Israel Beer hurried on this Passover night to his captivity.

At 9 p.m., he departed from his joyless flat at 67 Brandeis Street, Tel Aviv, where no Passover meal had been prepared to celebrate the departure of the Children of Israel from Egypt. He clasped a black document case under his right arm. Out of the open windows on this warm spring night wafted the songs of freedom as every family gathering chanted different portions of the Haggadah.

"This is the bread of affliction which our forefathers ate in the land of Egypt. Let all who are hungry come and eat, let all who are in need come and celebrate the Passover. Here and next year in the Land of Israel..."

Israel Beer walked rapidly, looking behind him. Out of a nearby window rang the high-pitched singsong of a boy. *"Ma Nishtana Halailah Hazeh?"* What is the difference between this night and all other nights...?

Israel Beer quickened his pace, looking behind him again and peering across the street. He turned at the next corner, hurried to a darkened newsstand, and stopped to catch his breath.

"We were slaves of Pharaoh in Egypt. But the Lord our God brought us forth from there with a strong hand and outstretched arm." An elder was recounting the age-old drama of the Exodus and Israel Beer caught the words from a Seder table brightly lit in the nearby apartment building.

Walking as if pursued by the chariots of Pharaoh, Israel Beer tightened his hold on his document case, and approached an obscure, run-down cafe that had remained open on this holiday night. Before ducking in, he looked back and to each side again.

Nodding to the only occupant, the owner, Israel Beer chose to sit at the table in the rear, least exposed to the pale neon light at the entrance.

"Cognac," he grunted. His hand shook as he lit a cigarette.

The cafe owner, himself a loner who chose to keep his place open this night of nights rather than sit alone, friendless in his own cheerless room, placed the small glass before the tall, thin customer who seldom talked although he frequently dropped in for a drink.

If elongated Beer had not been so skinny, he would have been described as a giant. His slender frame, high cheekbones dominating his gaunt face, marred by large, protruding upper teeth, twisted into a cadaverous grimace when he reflected pleasure, gave him a striking formidable appearance. His egg-shaped head was nearly bald, except for a sparse crown of clipped grey hair. A thin greyish mustache twitched with the nervous movements of his jaundiced, saturnine lips. At 49, he looked older by twenty years.

Gulping his cognac with a heavy heart, depressed by the soporific drowsiness of the dimly-lit cafe, Beer waited with wearisome foreboding.

21

Within five minutes, a man entered. Wearing a dark suit and a broad-brimmed grey felt hat, partly hiding his face, he moved unhesitatingly toward the occupied table, picked up the document case on the chair next to Beer, and without a word, turned around and walked out of the cafe.

Israel Beer looked at the disappearing figure, slowly disentangled himself from the chair, strolled to the cash register, plunked a single Pound on the counter, muttered a friendless "Shalom" to the owner, and ambled out into the street.

Emerging into the semi-darkness, he was greeted by the strains of Passover festivities from the open windows.

Intent upon his own thoughts, he could not help hearing a snatch of Seder service at this window, a song at that apartment, a chorus of singing at another.

"...In every generation in turn they rise up against us to destroy us."

"And the Egyptians ill treated us and they tormented us..."

"And the Lord brought us forth from Egypt with a mighty hand and with an outstretched arm..."

"And the Lord brought the great plagues upon the whole land of Egypt... Blood, Frogs, Lice, Wild Beasts, Pestilence, Boils, Hail, Locusts, Darkness, Slaying of the First-Born."

The joyous shouts of the *Dayenu* at his neighbors' house did not cheer Israel Beer as he returned home, stopped near the entrance, looked around and furtively sneaked in.

The Case of Beer

Precisely at midnight, Beer left his apartment again, carefully locked the door, and jogged down the steps to the front entrance. He glanced anxiously to the left and right, and ventured out into the street. The Passover feast had been concluded. The final hymn had already punctuated the night air. All was quiet. Most windows were darkened. He retraced his steps toward the cafe, now blacked out, shuttered.

As he approached the cafe, a car drove up behind him, and then stopped beside him, its motor running. The driver opened the door, alighted, and in a few steps was at Israel Beer's side. The driver handed the black document case to Beer. They looked into each other's face in the blackness of night. Not a word passed.

The driver, in dark suit and broad-brimmed grey felt hat, jumped back into his car, raced the engine, and sped away.

Beer put the document case under his arm, turned and hurried back toward his home. Instinct told him he was being followed, invisible eyes had witnessed the wordless delivery beside the automobile.

Cold sweat wetted his high forehead. Hands shaking, tightening his hold on his load of documents, he walked as fast as he could without breaking into a giveaway run. Without looking in any direction, he bolted upstairs into his house, and swore at the delay as his trembling hand repeatedly missed the keyhole. After seconds that seemed hours, he opened the door and shut it behind him. He had left the light on.

He entered his library and slumped into an armchair,

still holding the case of documents. All around him were bookshelves, laden to the ceiling with volumes printed in ten languages.

Hardly had he settled down and his heartbeat returned to near normal when he heard a sharp, commanding knock at his door.

Frozen in his armchair, fearing the worst, knowing that the inevitable moment had come, he waited for the knocking to stop, certain it would not. He suddenly was drained of the power to arouse himself and get up to open the door.

The knocking continued, for what seemed like ages, louder, insistent, until it sounded like a battering ram instead of an ordinary knock. The door lock broke loose. A husky officer of the Security Services burst in. Others followed and surrounded the lank, hatchet-faced figure slumped in the armchair, still holding the document case. The officer in charge took the case out of Beer's hands and snapped, "Israel Beer, you are under arrest. We have a search warrant."

"Go on. Do your duty," lamely answered the shadowy, scraggy Beer.

Disregarding Beer's invitation, the chief opened the document case, dumped its contents on the desk. Out dropped the notebooks in which Prime Minister David Ben Gurion meticulously wrote his private diary.

In these notebooks were the secrets of State and the innermost thoughts written in the cramped longhand of Israel's founding father-Defense Minister-scholar-author.

Who was Israel Beer? The shocked people of Israel

did not have to ask this question when the story of his arrest was released for publication ten days later.

Informed of Israel Beer's duplicity, David Ben Gurion moaned to his staff, "I lived surrounded by lies."

The Israeli public knew the name of Israel Beer. He was constantly mentioned in the press and was himself heard frequently on the State radio as a military commentator, as an adviser and trusted confidant in the Ministry of Defense, as a professor of military strategy and geo-political theory at the Israel war college, as official historian of the Israel Defense Forces, and military correspondent of the Labor Party newspaper, *Davar*.

The man in the street, leaning on Israel Beer's military expertise in the press and on the radio, and hearing of his close ties to the nation's leader who held the two most important posts of Prime Minister and Defense Minister, regarded the ubiquitous expert as a power behind the scenes. A reserve colonel in the Israel Army, Beer's functions in the Defense Ministry as official historian and adviser opened the confidential classified files to his prying eyes.

As the Beer case later unfolded to the public view, it was learned that the Passover night meeting at the neighborhood cafe was between Colonel (Reserve) Israel Beer and a member of the staff of the Soviet Union Embassy in Tel Aviv, known to Israeli counter-espionage as Russia's number one secret agent in the Jewish State.

Why Israel Beer betrayed the State of Israel, how he justified his double dealing in his own mind, how he came to this end, what was the strange story of his life ... all this was revealed in his own book written in prison.

Sentenced by a Jerusalem court in the summer of 1962 to serve fifteen years behind bars, Beer received permission in Shatta prison near the Jordan Valley to write his memoirs. His book, "Israel's Security, Yesterday, Today, Tomorrow," was published in Hebrew in 1966 shortly after his fatal heart attack in prison.

Beer's autobiography attempted to explain the rationale for his dealings with the Soviet Union.

Born October 9, 1912 in Vienna, Israel Beer was reared in a household of assimilated Jews, representative of the middle-class who believed that by denying their Jewish faith, they would gain entry and acceptance into gentile society and business success.

Israel Beer's parents, Henry and Anna Beer, were restless people who emigrated from Hungary to the United States, were unable to strike roots in the Golden Land and returned to Europe and finally settled down in the Austrian capital, the gay center of music and culture before the First World War shattered the Viennese illusion.

Too young to remember World War I, Israel Beer started school at the end of the conflict and graduated with honors from the Real Gymnasium Stubenbastei in 1930.

Enrolling at the University of Vienna, he came under the magnetic influence of Max Reinhardt, the famous dramatist and theater director. Young Beer decided upon the theater as a career, then selected the cinema as his special area. He was accepted for training in cinematography at the U.F.A. Film Studios in Berlin in 1932.

While still a student, he began to write for the *Berliner Tageblatt,* one of the great German newspapers of the pre-Hitler era.

Printers' ink got into the student's blood stream and lured him away from motion pictures. Passionately involved in the excitement of newspaper work and taking a keen interest in Germany's political controversies, Israel Beer was an eyewitness observer to the turbulent rise of Adolf Hitler.

Fleeing Germany when the Nazis came to power in 1933, Beer returned to Vienna where he threw himself into politics, choosing the Social Democratic Party for his vehicle. He joined a circle of left wing intellectuals led by Dr. Otto Bauer, a theoretician of classical socialism.

Beer returned to the University of Vienna, changing to courses in German Literature and Contemporary History for his major studies. He wrote his doctorate thesis on "The Way of Life, Culture and Art during the Rise and Fall of the Roman Middle Class."

From this lofty pinnacle of scholarly research, Dr. Beer descended to the street fights of Austrian revolutionary politics. He joined the "self-defense troops" of the Social Democratic Party, receiving his first military training with a student unit, The Academic Legion. When the Vienna working class revolted in a vain effort to break the Dollfuss dictatorship, Dr. Beer fought shoulder to shoulder with the workers against the state police and army forces, according to his own account.

It was a short-lived rebellion that started on February

12, 1934. The workers fought with pistols, rifles and stones from behind barricades and the walls of the Social Democratic Party headquarters building at Ottakring in a suburb of Vienna. After two days of one-sided fighting, the workers' ranks broke under the intensive bombardment of Austrian Army artillery; they surrendered on February 14th. Beer was among the fighters who escaped capture by hiding in the sewer system.

The experience of defeat taught the Doctor of German Literature at the age of twenty-two that the victory of socialism would have to be achieved by military strength and prowess rather than in parlor discussions and scholarly articles. He crossed party lines to enroll in the military training school sponsored by the Fascist-oriented Government. He recalled that he was not asked his political affiliations or his religion, and he kept secret both his recent revolutionary combat activity and his Jewish background. The anti-Semitic Dollfuss regime barred Jews from the army and the civil administration. Dr. Beer claimed that he passed the course in para-military training at Bruck and was assigned with his military schoolmates to help defend the capital when the National Socialists assassinated Premier Dollfuss. Beer said his unit recaptured the radio station after it had been taken by a band of armed Nazis. As he told it, he won the admiration of his superiors and was recommended for officer training school. Passing the officers' course with flying colors, Beer was advanced to the Austrian Military Academy at Wiener-Neustadt where he received his commission as lieutenant in 1935. Posted to the Third Infantry

Division, Lieutenant Beer arranged a transfer to the Government Militia, and then to the Shock Militia.

To Lieutenant Beer, there was no inner confiict between being a Doctor of Philosophy in German Literature, and an officer in the Austrian Shock Militia, between believing in socialism and serving in the Fascist Army.

He lived a double life, fulfilling his duties in uniform with the Shock Militia, while conducting an active political role in civilian clothes when he was off duty. In the political underground, he gravitated to the extreme left wing of the outlawed Socialists, formerly the Social Democratic Party.

This was the time when the Spanish Civil War was brewing, and the beleaguered Republican Army appealed for volunteers from other countries. The Socialist militants where Beer found himself among ideological comrades volunteered to join the International Brigade, and the story goes that Beer accompanied them first to Switzerland, then to Paris.

According to Beer's account, he met Tito when the Yugoslav President-to-be was a young director of volunteer recruiting in Paris for the International Brigade. Tito sent Beer's group of Viennese Socialists to Albacete, headquarters of the Brigade. Beer said he was promoted to instructor on the strength of his Austrian military experience and rank. He instructed raw recruits on how to fire automatic weapons.

Flaunting his lieutenant's rank and his Doctor of Philosophy degree, he ingratiated himself into the circles of

International Brigade officers. Among his new-found friends were Wilfred MacCartney, Commander of the First Regiment, and Tom Wintrigham, Commander of the British Battalion, both well known London Communist Leaders.

Beer always liked to tell stories of the battles of Madrid and Guadalajara where he pictured himself as commander of a company of the Edgar Andre Battalion. Later he was promoted to the command of the Hans Beimler Battalion. He claimed to have been a staff officer of Hans Kahle, who replaced the famed "Gen. Gomez," in real life Wilhelm Zaisser. Kahle's Chief-of-Staff was the Communist writer, Ludwig Renn.

As the Spanish War raged on, Beer was given command of a mixed German-Spanish battalion which fought in the Battle of Brunette, west of Madrid in the summer of 1937. There, Beer collaborated with a young Russian armored force colonel, Ivan Koniev, destined to rise to eminence as a Soviet Marshal in World War II.

Beer's story of his war achievements included distinguished service in the battle of Catalonia, with subsequent reward in promotion to the General Staff of the Karl Marx Division, commanded by a Soviet general known by the *nom de guerre* of Walter. He imagined himself to be moving up and up in the estimation of the Russian generals who named the intrepid Austrian fighter as adviser to the Republican Army General Staff. In that role, Commander Beer devised a new infiltration strategy which worked effectively in the Battle of Elbro in 1938.

Taking Beer at his word, he was an intimate of such

legendary commanders as Lazlo Rajk, General Julius Deutsch, and the generals of the Twelfth and Thirteenth International Brigades who hid their identities under false names. Beer himself was known by the aliases of Captain Jose Gregorio or Commander Miguel Diaz.

When the International Brigade was disbanded in 1938, the Russian Generals, Gouriev and Griszin, who had taken a liking to the young Austrian, offered Beer a chance to go to the Soviet Union for advanced military training in the Red Army Academy. They regarded Beer as a faithful Marxist and saw in him the makings of a representative for service to the Soviet in its external operations.

In Paris, Soviet agents supplied Beer with faked identity papers, with orders to proceed to Czechoslovakia via Switzerland. En route, he was to spend a month with his parents in Vienna, and wind up his personal affairs.

Back home, he had a chance to think about his imaginary Spanish war experiences. Dazzled by the glamour surrounding the Russian Spanish Republican cause to the fact that the Soviet intervention was motivated by Stalin's desire to test his weapons and his army officers in combat, and not a sincere regard for the freedom and welfare of the Spanish people who bore the agony of the Civil War only to fall under the Fascist dictatorship of Generalissimo Franco.

As Beer pondered the reasons for the defeat of the cause which he identified with, he became disillusioned with Stalinism and he changed his mind about going to Moscow.

So his story went.

As he told it to friends in later years and reviewed it in his autobiography, his change of heart was precipitated by a chance impulse to read the biography of Theodor Herzl, founder of Zionism. Fascinated by the idea of the return of the Jews to their ancestral homeland in Palestine, Beer, who had never shown any interest before in Zionism, compulsively read book after book about the Jews in Palestine, Jewish history and the Jewish religion.

His socialist theories were being put into practice in Jewish Palestine by the thriving workers' cooperatives, the kibbutzim, and the Histadrut, without resorting to the authoritarianism of the Russian Communists. He had come to the conclusion that the national liberation movement of the Jewish people had a profound meaning in international terms.

Deciding to go to Jerusalem instead of Moscow, Beer registered with the Hechalutz Zionist pioneering organization in Vienna which assisted immigration to the Holy Land.

The grotesque story of how Israel Beer had to retrieve his identity papers in order to go on Aliyah is one of those chapters in his autobiography which may be read with incredulity, probably one of his imaginative flights of invention.

He claimed to have entrusted his identity papers with the office of the Austrian Socialist Democratic Party before departing for Spain. The papers, as was the custom in the Nazi period, were loaned to a young Jewish intellectual to enable him to escape from the Hitler Storm Troops in Berlin to temporary haven in Vienna, while awaiting his immigration certificate to Haifa.

Soon after Beer's return from Spain, the Nazis occupied Austria, and his own predicament was aggravated by lack of identity papers. The Nazi occupiers were making wholesale round-ups of suspected Communists, Socialists and fellow travelers. Without identity papers, he was doomed if arrested. Even with identity papers, he was in danger if the Nazis learned of his leftish sympathies in Austria and Spain.

The extremist organization, which had arranged his Spanish interlude, wanted him to fulfill his promises to go to Moscow. He was offered the bleak choice: We will replace your identity papers if you go to the U.S.S.R. If you refuse to go, you will be without identification.

Faced with this dilemma, Beer recalled that he confronted the intellectual who was using the name of Israel Beer and demanded the return of his own identity papers. The young man, whose life hinged on retaining Beer's papers, adamantly refused. Beer implied years later that he killed the man using his name.

Beer escaped and reinforced with his own papers made his way to an immigration camp where he joined a group of refugees fleeing from the Nazis to find new lives in Jewish Palestine.

He arrived in Haifa in November 1938 and took up residence in Jerusalem. There he volunteered for service in the Jewish civilian defense, organized by the British

Mandatory Government, to protect outlying Jewish settlements against attacks by Arab brigands.

One of his favorite stories is about the British officer who directed him to guard his jeep.

"I did not graduate from the Austrian Military Academy to watch over your jeep." Beer defiantly replied.

The Englishman was astounded at such insolence, but inwardly impressed, and so he asked Beer to tell him more details about his military experience. Beer, never bashful about his exploits, real or imagined, told the officer about his rank of lieutenant in the Austrian Shock Militia, and his rise to lieutenant colonel in the Spanish Republican Army. He also boasted of his Doctor of Philosophy degree in German Literature. The officer noted the name of Israel Beer and in a few days, the hero of Austria and Spain was transferred out of Jewish civilian defense into the German Department of British Intelligence in Jerusalem.

The Jewish Agency, then the "shadow" government of the Jewish community, had eyes and ears in every British office and learned that a Jew had been installed in the Mandatory Government Intelligence Service.

Beer received a secret visit from the Hebrew underground defense organization, Haganah, which enlisted him into its own intelligence branch as a double agent, working both for the British and the Jews.

By 1940, Beer had painted such an impressive image of his Austrian and Spanish achievements to everyone within earshot that the Haganah Command decided to send him to the underground officers training course at the Kadoorie Agricultural School near the Sea of Galilee.

An Israeli general later recalled Israel Beer's arrival at Kadoorie, located in the shadow of Mount Tabor.

"Beer wore shorts which accentuated the dreadful thinness of his bow-legs. He carried an Alpinist's Tyrolean knapsack. He looked neither like a veteran of the Spanish Civil War nor like a possible future Israeli Army commander. I put him to the test for one day. It was plain to me that this man had no real military or combat experience. It was all a lie. He might be a genius at tactics, but as a soldier he was worthless.

"Here, take a book, catch the next bus and go back to Jerusalem," I told Beer. He said nothing and went away. I don't think Israel Beer ever held a gun in his hands, before then and after then."

Years later, the general attended a lecture on Israel's security problems. The "expert" lecturer proved to be— none other than Israel Beer.

Rejected for the Haganah officers' course, Beer was undaunted and offered his services to the underground organization's newspaper as a writer on tactics and strategy. Written in German, his articles were translated into Hebrew and published under the byline of Dr. I. Beer or the pen name, I. Ben Israel.

Impressed by his articles and his courtly manner and the embellishments of his imaginary military feats, the Jewish Agency leaders assigned him to edit technical and theoretical reviews of foreign military translations for the Haganah officers' corps.

The Agency officials, with their own cultural roots

mainly in Eastern Europe, joked about the "Yecke" with his grand tales of the Spanish Civil War.

Beer's military articles made him well known in the Haganah and Agency circles, and he capitalized on his prominence by ingratiating himself with the leaders of the "shadow" government who were to become the cabinet ministers and the generals of the Jewish State to be.

His reputation was enhanced by his position as military correspondent of *Davar*, the newspaper organ of the ruling Labour Party, and the voice of Histadrut.

Among his close friends whose ears he pounded with military theory and geopolitical concepts were Eliahu Golomb, founder of Haganah; Yacov Dori, who was to become Israel's first Chief-of-Staff; Yigal Yadin, Chief of Operations during the War of Independence; and Yigal Allon, the foremost field commander of the 1948 War of Independence, who was destined to rise to political eminence. The legendary Yitzhak Sadeh, one of Haganah's greatest pre-war leaders, spent many hours in Beer's company as they discussed defense problems and socialist ideology.

During World War II, Beer wrote regularly in *Davar*, interpreting the course of the great conflict upon which hinged the fate of Jewish Palestine, especially when Rommel's Afrika Korps threatened at one time to break through the last Allied defenses in Egypt and drive to the shores of Palestine.

During this phase of the North African campaign, Israel Beer delivered a series of lectures on the desert war to the Haganah commanders. Perhaps as a result of his alleged expertise, as he wrote and spoke on warfare with self-confident authority, he was appointed Chief of Operations for Haganah in Upper Galilee. This was at the beginning of 1945, when the Jewish community already was planning ahead to the end of World War II, preparing the campaign to establish a Jewish Commonwealth, and girding for the possibility that the Arabs would attack the Jewish settlements.

Beer participated in drawing up contingency plans for defense of the northern area. With headquarters in Haifa, Beer at one time was a commanding figure throughout the Galilee. True to form he had found a ravishing beauty to be his secretary in Haifa, and having divorced his first wife, had married the ex-wife of his secretary's new husband! Beer left his second wife a few years after their marriage, and although they were never divorced, he openly lived with another woman.

On the eve of the 1948 War of Independence, Beer was transferred to Haganah headquarters in Tel Aviv where he served on the General Staff under Generals Dori and Yadin with David Ben Gurion in overall control of war preparations and operations.

Beer, promoted to colonel, survived Ben Gurion's ruthless liquidation of the Palmach striking force and its consolidation, along with the Irgun Zvai Leumi and Stern Gang underground units, into one single Israel Defense Force, known in Hebrew as Zva Haganah Le Israel, or Israel Defense Force.

He emerged from the reorganization retaining his colonelcy in Zahal.

He was known throughout the country for his newspaper articles, probably one of the most prominent officers in Israel where anonymity was a rite among army men except at the highest ranks. Beer relished the glamor of his natty uniform and his colonel's epaulets. His three-room apartment in Tel Aviv was a meeting place of high ranking officers, cabinet ministers, director-generals, diplomats, artists and editors. A gourmet, he prepared his sumptuous meals for his guests. A sparkling conversationalist, Colonel Beer exuded *joie de vivre,* as he stimulated exciting discussions around his table of delicacies.

He regaled his dinner parties with fables of the Spanish Civil War, there being no other veterans of the Republican-Loyalist conflict in Israel to challenge his mythical anecdotes.

His great German shepherd dog, Azza, always at his feet, the resplendent colonel entertained the elite with comic caricatures of Russian generals commanding Spanish peasants in the International Brigades. The witty colonel's ferocious German accent of his awkward Hebrew enhanced the fun.

At one of his home soirees, when the wine and the whiskey were spreading conviviality, Colonel Beer confided in his companions: "Imagine what I would have become had I followed the advice of my friends in the International Brigade and gone from Spain to the Soviet Union! I might have become a Red Army general and then Stalin would have sent me to Siberia or put me up against a firing squad, like so many other high officers with Spanish War experience. Reading Herzl saved my life. In Spain I knew Marshal Constantin Rokossowsky like a brother. He was a romantic, he hated war. I once gave him a bawling out for shirking his duty during intensive fighting on our front. When Rokossowsky returned to Moscow from Spain, Stalin had him jailed. He stayed in prison until the Second World War. Then Stalin remembered he had an experienced general in prison, and rehabilitated Rokossowsky who became one of the great Red Army heroes. He was lucky to survive Stalin's purge of hundreds of army officers."

By the end of the War of Independence, Colonel Beer had risen to Chief of the Planning Branch of the General Staff. Suddenly, without public explanations, he was out of uniform.

His unexplained farewell to arms appeared to be due to a political miscalculation on his part, a mistake which surprised his friends who respected his clever, astute maneuvering of the intricate highways and byways of Israeli power. From the beginning of his meteoric career in Jewish Palestine, he aligned himself with the dominant Mapai party, led by Ben Gurion, the controlling power in the Jewish Agency and the Histadrut under the British regime. If this was political opportunism for a former Viennese Socialist at the most extreme militant left, it paid off handsomely with the accruements of privilege and position.

Mapai, an amalgam of labor groups without a dynamic ideology, was guided by the pragmatic Ben Gurion, to whom the State was always paramount, with the party and the workers' class playing subsidiary roles to the primacy of the nation. Dissenting from Ben Gurion's "statism," splinter groups dedicated to their socialist ideologies split off from Mapai in the never-ending amoebic processes of Israeli politics.

Falling under the influence of Dr. Moshe Sneh, onetime Haganah Chief-of-Staff and a brilliant leftist theoretician, Colonel Beer followed Sneh into the left-wing Mapam party.

This was heresy to Ben Gurion, for the "Mapamnicks" had seized upon the issue of the forced integration of the Palmach into the Israel Defense Forces as a political cause. Many of the commanders of Palmach came from these left-wing kibbutzim and regarded their elite shock troops as standing above and beyond the regular army, something akin to the historic status of the United States Marine Corps. Among the Palmach commanders, including heroes of countless battles with Arabs and British troops before the 1948 War, there was a school of thought that believed that Palmach should provide the model upon which the new Israel Army should be structured.

Ben Gurion disagreed with these great fighting commanders and insisted on a regular army, a unified army. Even the Air Force and the Navy were unified in the Israel Defense Forces under a single Chief-of-Staff and General Staff. Ben Gurion categorically rejected the Palmach ideal of an ideological army, with independent status, based upon the hard core of the working class, the kibbutzim and the cooperatives. Ben Gurion pushed through his army reorganization, demanding one army, built upon rank, merit, discipline and technological development. Palmach officers who refused to abide by Ben Gurion's orders were allowed to resign and return to private life. General Yigal Allon, Palmach's leading commander and outstanding field general of the War of Independence, left the army after the victory which he helped win, and organized the Achdut Haavodah party with Generals Moshe Carmel and Israel Galili.

Colonel Beer, following Sneh into Mapam, is believed to have been motivated not by a concern for Palmach but by opportunism, on the assumption—erroneous as it later proved to be—that in a small splinter party, he stood a better chance of reaching the top rung of political power than in the large, amorphous Mapai Party ruled by Ben Gurion.

As Dr. Sneh veered farther and farther to the left, until he finally quit Mapam to take the leadership of the Communist Party and edit its daily newspaper, *Kol Haam,* Beer realized his mistake and tried to retrace his steps back into Mapai, which retained the seats of power in election after election.

Ousted from Mapam for "leftist deviationism," Beer issued a public declaration in the press that the only possible way of insuring the country's future in a socialist context was through the Mapai party and the leadership of Prime Minister David Ben Gurion.

Beer's publicized recantation in 1953 paved the ground for his return to Mapai, but he found the road back to the army blocked by Isser Harel, chief of Israeli Secret Services. Harel had read an article by Israel Beer in a

left-wing newspaper in which the Korean War was analyzed in terms hostile toward the United States participa-
tion, while the Soviet stand was treated with understanding and approval. Harel read between the lines and suspected Beer's extreme leftist thinking at a time when
Moscow was drawing closer to the Arab side and cooling
its relations with Jerusalem.

Harel vetoed Beer's return to a responsible General
Staff position, and was supported by the ascendant young
commanders, led by Moshe Dayan, who were unim-
pressed by the European military background of a passe
school. The Dayan generation of army leaders looked
ahead and were determined not to fight the next war with
the weapons and tactics of the past war, and certainly not
to be influenced by a self-styled expert from the Spanish
Civil War of a decade and a half ago.

General Dayan, slated to be the next Chief-of-Staff,
dismissed Beer in Sabra-fashion: "He read a lot but learned nothing." Dayan, a direct, clear-thinking farmer from
Nahalal, had no time or sympathy for Beer's Viennese
sleekness and grandiloquent circumlocutions.

Finding the Army High Command closed to him,
Beer tried another tack. He resurrected his pre-war work
as a Haganah journalist and won a post in the Ministry
of Defense as editor of a military history of the War of
Independence. The Defense Ministry Director-General,
Shimon Peres, also entrusted Beer with preparing strategic
studies.

The military history of the War of Independence was
never completed by Beer, but he published extracts of

his work which highlighted the wartime leadership of Ben Gurion and thus healed his political rift with the Prime Minister.

Beer sliced through the polemics of Ben Gurion's controversy with the Palmach commanders over their group's dissolution. He recanted his previous advocacy of a permanent Palmach and admitted that Ben Gurion was right from the beginning. The creation of the parachutists' corps within the new Israel Defense Forces was in the tradition of the Palmach striking force, but it was an integrated part and parcel of I.D.F., and completely under the command of the General Staff. Beer extolled the Ben Gurion retaliation policy as it was beginning to develop in the early 1950's when the paratroop units struck hard at Arab terrorist hideouts across the Jordan border.

When Moshe Dayan was promoted by Ben Gurion to Chief-of-Staff, Beer was regarded as the theoretician of the activist policy being carried out. Beer wrote newspaper articles justifying the Ben Gurion-Dayan-Peres retaliation doctrine, which was being questioned abroad and in some dissident circles at home.

Notwithstanding Beer's restoration of his popular image as an interpreter of the policies of the administration and as a member of the "team," Isser Harel remained suspicious and uneasy about the army historian who had regained access to the innermost secrets of Israel's defense.

Isser Harel kept watch on Israel Beer.

CHAPTER TWO

BEER MEETS "MR. X"

During Ben Gurion's self-imposed exile to his Sde Boker kibbutz in 1955, deep in the Negev, when he temporarily yielded the Premiership to Moshe Sharett, Israel Beer made several journeys to the desert outpost for long, confidential talks with the nation's founding father.

According to Beer's autobiography, Ben Gurion expressed doubts about the directions of foreign policy. The Egyptian-Czechoslovak arms deal marked a reversal of Soviet Middle East policy away from support of Israel to arming and building up Nasser's army. This signalized the start of Russian penetration into the Mediterranean region, the reawakening of an ancient Czarist dream hundreds of years old.

Beer's version of his conversations with Ben Gurion leaves the impression that the old statesman-scholar was not adverse to countering the imbalance created by Soviet backing of Egypt by attempting a rapprochement with Moscow, rather than placing all of Israel's eggs in the basket of commitment to the West.

Beer, predicting the deepening involvement of Soviet

power in the Middle East, with its dangers to Israel's security, advanced the thesis that Israel could only be saved from the Russian menace by helping to establish a Jewish-Arab Federation under the Communist powers' trusteeship. Ben Gurion told Beer, according to the latter's reports, that he was not opposed to engaging in a dialogue with the Soviets, but he felt that Moscow first should show some token of good will towards Jerusalem.

In contrast to his newspaper articles of the early 1950's extolling the Ben Gurion-Dayan-Peres activist approach, Beer in his autobiography written in prison criticized the retaliations in hindsight as leading to the 1956 Sinai War. Looking backward from his cell in Shatta, Beer, the convicted spy, wrote that Israel should have pursued a different policy of easing tensions to court favor with the Russians.

"The thaw had started three years earlier," Beer wrote in prison, "de-Stalinization had made notable advances under Khruschev. Already, the first signs of a 'Second October' were appearing in Poland and Hungary. In April 1955, Moscow had recommended to the Western Powers a neutralization of the Middle East, and a limitation of arms applying to the entire region. Soviet Foreign Minister Molotov, presenting this proposal for neutralization and arms limitation, declared in Geneva that the U.S.S.R. was supplying arms to Egypt strictly on a commercial basis, and any other country was free to do the same."

Beer then brought his ideas into the open for an Eastern reorientation of Israeli foreign policy. As one of the spokesmen for the Defense Ministry assigned to brief visiting writers, Beer expounded his theories to representatives of the foreign press as well as to his friends among the Israeli journalists. He sought out acquaintances among the resident correspondents for foreign newspapers and agencies and propounded his ideas for outside dissemination.

In the autumn of 1956, several weeks before the outbreak of the Sinai War, Beer met with a member of an East European Embassy in Tel Aviv, later identified as "Mr. X." The meeting came to the attention of Ben Gurion's aide-de-camp, Colonel Nehemia Argov, who advised Beer to report the conversation to the Chief of counter-espionage. Beer followed Colonel Argov's advice and was informed coldly by the head counter-spy that "Mr. X" was engaged in espionage in Israel.

"Beer, you are strictly forbidden to have any contacts with this spy," the Chief told him.

Ignoring his explicit instructions, Beer arranged a luncheon date with "Mr. X" and they spent a long afternoon together.

On September 28, 1956, exactly a month before the Sinai War, Beer was called in by the Chief of Israel Intelligence and informed that he had met a certain person against the advice of Colonel Argov and the Chief of counter-espionage. The Intelligence Chief repeated to Beer that he was under strict orders not to see that person again.

Did Israel Beer expose Israel's closest-guarded secret about plans to launch a pre-emptive strike against Egypt in connection with the British-French Suez invasion?

Beer claimed in his defense that he knew nothing in advance about the military plans for the Sinai Campaign, as it was called in Israel. Occupying a sensitive position in the Defense Ministry, could he have been unaware of the secret trips to France being made by Ben Gurion, Dayan, Peres and others? Was he oblivious to stepped up activity in the Defense Ministry, increased armament deliveries from France, and military movements?

Something was up. The time of the operation, and the direction it would take, was a secret so tightly kept by General Dayan and the General Staff that many officers heading southward on the day of the invasion thought they were on a diversionary mission to cover an actual attack on Jordan which had been the source of terrorist assaults against Israeli settlements.

It was possible, despite Beer's denials, that he knew enough to tip off "Mr. X" that something was brewing, although he could not in all probability have been privy to the secret of the Sinai plans. When Israeli paratroops dropped on Mitla Pass on October 29, 1956, it was a total surprise to the Egyptian High Command and their Soviet suppliers.

Israel's lightning rout of the Egyptian Army in Sinai did not change Beer's mind about the Soviet threat to the nation's future security. As Moscow and Washington jointly exerted pressure upon Jerusalem to withdraw from the Sinai Peninsula, Beer felt that his ideas had been vindicated. Israel indeed stood alone, without friends either in Washington or Moscow. France and Britain were disgraced in the Suez fiasco. As history later proved, France was a weak foundation upon which to base Israel's security although Paris continued to be Zahal's major supplier of vital defense weapons until 1967.

Beer found a kindred soul in Dr. Nahum Goldmann, president of both the World Zionist Organization and the World Jewish Congress, who shared his views and was later to adopt the idea of a neutralized Israel in a modified form. Goldmann was rumored to have offered Beer the editorship of a political review but the journalistic project never materialized.

Beer welcomed Goldmann's indirect parallelism of thought but discounted the Zionist leader as an active ally because of his organizational ties and his cautious personal diplomacy.

The outcome of the Sinai War convinced Beer that, in his words, "I must launch a campaign of personal diplomacy to save Israel from inevitable historical cataclysm." He defined the reasons for his decision:

"1. There is no possibility that in the near future Israel will formulate a serious, durable alternative to the pro-Western foreign policy initiated by Ben Gurion.

"2. Ben Gurion's foreign policy will lead Israel to eventual isolation, facing a united hostile Arab world, supported by Soviet power, which threatens the third destruction of the Jewish Commonwealth in history.

"3. A lone individual does not stand a chance to carry out a successful campaign aimed at warding off the Arab-Soviet menace closing in on Israel.

"4. Notwithstanding this handicap, I am under a

moral obligation to do all in my limited power to try to change our foreign policy and avert the threat of destruction.

71-778

"5. Conscious of this personal responsibility for Israel's future, and confident that I possess the intellectual qualities and moral authority, I take it upon myself to labor for the ultimate salvation of Israel, without having been charged by constituted authorities with that mission. The risk is my own. The choice is mine alone. I hope the results will justify the means."

Beer arranged through his contacts with Communist countries to be invited to European capitals for a series of lectures on the Middle East situation. This afforded him a cover for contacts both outside and behind the Iron Curtain.

During frequent trips to Europe that followed in the years 1957 to 1960, he met many Communist diplomats and representatives. His expressed aim was to bring to Israel a group of personalities from the Soviet Union and the Eastern European satellites. He would make a study of the conditions in Israel and the Middle East which would motivate their Communist countries to change their policies towards the Jewish State.

Starting with Eastern European diplomats stationed in Tel Aviv and Jerusalem, Beer unfolded his grandiose ideas. They encouraged him, and arranged for the lecture tours.

In West Germany, Beer was publicized as one of Israel's foremost military experts. One general labeled him, "Israel's Liddell-Hart." He was invited to address veterans' organizations and military academies who were impressed with Israel's blitzkrieg victory in the Sinai War.

According to Beer's story, he met once again with old friends from the Spanish Civil War days, who had since risen to important positions in their respective countries.

In his contacts with Communist representatives, he arranged for two-way activity. He would promote his pro-Eastern views in Israel. They would seek to improve Israel-Soviet relationships. It was decided that in Tel Aviv, he would maintain contact with the Communist Bloc through only one person, a "Mr. Y," the member of an Eastern European Embassy.

Beer agreed to provide information on political developments, and the progress of his personal diplomatic campaign, through "Mr. Y."

After a final meeting in Tel Aviv with "Mr. X," Beer had frequent contacts with "Mr. Y," both at his Brandeis Street apartment, and in cafes and other rendezvous, where reports and documents were passed hand to hand.

In 1960, Beer made a trip to West Germany and crossed the Berlin Wall to hold a secret session in East Berlin, and then fly to an undisclosed Communist capital. On his return, he met in Bonn with a West German key government official. The Israel Embassy learned of the conference. The word was flashed to Israel Intelligence. Isser Harel suspected Beer of engaging in underground activity on behalf of the Communist Bloc, not only harmful to Israel but also to another power friendly to Jerusalem.

With his credentials as an official in the Israel Defense

Ministry, Israel Beer was in a position to procure confidential information in West Germany concerning NATO military developments, and pass them on through his Eastern European contacts to the Soviet Union.

Harel warned Ben Gurion of this possibility, informing the Prime Minister about Beer's travels and meetings with Eastern European emissaries. Apparently, Ben Gurion dismissed Harel's suspicions and made no move to relieve the army historian from his sensitive post where he had access to classified information dealing with defense matters.

By the autumn of 1960, Harel ordered a constant watch on Beer's movements.

"After my return from Europe in 1960, I felt I was being watched. I complained about it to Ben Gurion's aide-de-camp, Colonel Argov, who told me not to worry," Beer later recalled.

In February 1961, Beer prepared a series of articles for *The Jerusalem Post* on Ben Gurion as a personality, a nation-builder, and creative molder of national defense and foreign policy. To provide him with primary source material, Beer was permitted to see Ben Gurion's private diary, written by hand, in small rectangular notebooks. Studying the diary, Beer found passages which he thought substantiated his basic thesis that the Prime Minister was not basically anti-Soviet or anti-Communist, and therefore was flexible enough to reorient his foreign policy in the eastward direction favored by the army historian.

Beer was anxious to prove his contention to the Eastern European emissaries with whom he had been in touch. He phoned "Mr. Y" on March 26, 1961. They arranged an appointment in the small cafe near his home. "Mr. Y" failed to keep the appointment. Beer called "Mr. Y" again. On March 27, they huddled over a beer. "Mr. Y" offered to make photocopies of the Ben Gurion diary within a few hours after receiving the notebooks. The next night was the first night of Passover. Normal activity would be suspended. Probably even the Intelligence people would be at their family *Seder* gatherings. They agreed to meet again in the same cafe on the first night of Passover when Beer would deliver the notebooks.

For Isser Harel this night was no different from other nights. Israel cannot afford to let down its guard against external or internal enemies. Harel's agents had been accumulating evidence against Beer, and the decision was made to spring the trap on him on Passover eve.

Either underestimating the vigilant watchfulness of the Security Services, or feeling that he was so deeply committed to his self-appointed mission that he must take any risk, Israel Beer on the first night of Passover disregarded the Haggadah and picked up Ben Gurion's diaries instead, placed them with other documents in his document case, and set out from his house for his fateful appointment with personal disaster.

Looking back on his arrest, Beer contended he was neither frightened nor surprised. His first reaction was to consider it only a passing incident, to be cleared up easily. Instinct told him that Isser Harel's animosity toward him, dating back through the entire decade of the 1950's, had now taken a serious turn. Sure that Security Services knew of his contacts with "Mr. Y," he assumed they would be introduced as evidence in court to prove his culpability. But Israel Beer was so obsessed with his righteousness, with the rightness of his grand design for Israel's national security, that he considered himself innocent of wrong-doing and demanded that his office at the Defense Ministry be informed immediately about his incarceration and that Shimon Peres and Colonel Argov be summoned to see him without delay.

Neither Peres nor Argov visited him in confinement. Neither the Prime Minister's Office nor the Defense Ministry intervened on his behalf. Crestfallen that he was abandoned by Ben Gurion and his closest friends in his hour of trial, Beer's self-confidence collapsed and he decided to confess. To his mind, however, confession did not mean truth. He would cooperate with the investigation and tell them stories, plagiarized from spy tales and detective novels, tailored to the requirements of the investigation. Had he said nothing, he figured that he would be liable to administrative detention for an undetermined period, according to the British Mandate regulations of the pre-1948 period still in effect.

The correctness of his personal diplomacy could only have been understood by a Ben Gurion who also thought in global concepts, Beer thought. Isser Harel and his investigators were incapable of understanding Beer's grand design for a new foreign policy. This was the logic of Israel Beer as he wove a web of deceit in answering his interlocutors.

It is wiser to tell some harmless espionage stories and

go to jail for a short term than refuse to talk and be held without trial in indefinite administrative detention, he reasoned. In jail, he would spend his time writing a great ideological work, demonstrating the errors of the Ben Gurionist foreign policy, and logically proving the case for a new Eastward direction for the salvation of Israel. So sure was he of the impregnability of his analysis that he fancied an overwhelming popular demand for his release as soon as his book was published and read. In the meanwhile, he would be sacrificing his personal freedom for the greater good of his country's long-term freedom and security.

In his confession, which he later described as "an invention from beginning to end," Beer also played on sympathy for himself. He stated: "I, a poor intellectual, allowed myself to be trapped. Little by little, without being aware of it, I let myself be drawn along the road of treason by a foreign agent. When I finally came to realize it, it was too late."

Beer wrote a letter to Ben Gurion, expressing the faith that when the magnus opus of a new foreign policy program was completed in prison, the great Prime Minister would understand. He did not expect the judges, however, to comprehend the magnitude of the service he had undertaken to assure the integrity of his country.

Within three months of his arrest on Passover 1961, Beer stood before the bar of justice in the Tel Aviv District Court. The verdict of the court was not handed down until January, 1962. The charge against him was that he had prejudiced the security of the State. The jurists stated in their verdict that in their opinion, the defendant's actions had not been treasonable in intent. He was sentenced to ten years in prison. Beer appealed to the Supreme Court whose three-jurist review of the Lower Court proceedings was not completed until the summer of 1962. The Supreme Court confirmed the findings of the Lower Court and increased the sentence from ten years to fifteen years. The Supreme Court found that Beer's initial contact with "Mr. X" laid the groundwork for a systematic program of actions that either gravely prejudiced the security of the State, or caused irreparable damage to the security of the State.

In adding five years to the ten-year sentence decreed by the District Court, the High Tribunal ruled that in Israel Beer's case, the supreme penalty of life imprisonment would be justified because "this man belonged to the Defense Ministry where he had access to secret information of a military and strategic value and passed it on to agents and spies of a foreign power which maintains the closest relations with the enemies of the State of Israel."

Writing in Shatta prison, Beer accused the courts of betraying the cause of justice, as he interpreted justice. He labeled the judicial decisions as "political judgments" and accused one of the judges of acting in collusion with the head of the Secret Services. He pictured himself as a man who never betrayed his country but sacrificed himself for Israel. "Everywhere I shall be, as a free man or in prison, I shall remain a loyal citizen and soldier of Israel," he wrote.

CHAPTER THREE

BEER THE BIG BLUFF

The investigation and the trial of Israel Beer exposed chapter after chapter of his oft-told life story to be a pack of lies, a masquerade of fabrication, fraud, perfidy and make-believe.

"Who were your parents?" he was asked.

"I remember nothing," he insisted, "I know nothing. In any event, they are dead."

Was he Jewish?

How could he prove it? He was uncircumcised, although the failure to observe the age-old Abrahamic rite was not uncommon among assimilated Jews of the first part of the twentieth century in Europe, who dreamt of acceptance among the gentiles, not perpetuation of the Jewish faith.

Investigation of the records of the Wiener-Neustadt Military Academy in Austria failed to find the name of Israel Beer among the cadets of his time. The Military Academy, in fact, discriminated against Jews in its acceptance policy. The "Schutz Bund" and the Vienna Social Democratic Party, to which Beer feigned allegiance, had no listing of his name.

At the University of Vienna, a meticulous examination could not locate him on a roster of doctoral candidates.

Beer's posture as a Spanish Civil War hero was more difficult to disprove because the war records of the Republican Army and its International Brigades were not cherished by the Franco Government. Yet, a careful reading of the vast literature written over the years by fighters in the Brigade concluded that Israel Beer or his aliases, Diaz and Gregorio, did not exist as a soldier or officer of any significance.

Faced with this negative report and cross-examined during the trial in the Tel Aviv District Court, Beer lifted his mask of sham and admitted the whole story of the Spanish Civil War was a forgery, a big lie.

"Did you go to Spain during the Civil War?" he was asked.

"To tell the truth," he replied, "I never set foot in Spain."

All the legerdemain about his name-dropping associations with the Russian generals, the concoction of a mirage of his tinsel military experience, the camouflage of his expertise on warfare, the deceit concerning his strategy and tactics, all this was bunk, hollow cant, a cunning trick to falsify himself as someone who could gain credence inside Israel's defense circles from the early Haganah days and on.

Grilled to pin him to his deceptions, he confessed that

during the Spanish War years, 1936 to 1939, he lived in Vienna until he immigrated to Palestine in 1938.

"Then why did you invent your Spanish War epic?" a jurist inquired of the bogus hero.

"The first time I told this story in Palestine," explained the confessed mountebank, "we used to argue here about the best way to get rid of the British. I was an activist. I supported all-out activity to make the existence of the Mandate unbearable for them. I returned to my classical Marxist analysis based on the inevitable struggle of the working class against imperialism. I regretted that I had not joined the International Brigade in Spain. I couldn't admit that I had failed to commit myself to that struggle for liberty against dictatorship in Spain. So I started to tell my friends that I did fight in Spain, and I elaborated on the story as time went on. This gave me some inner satisfaction."

"Sort of auto-suggestion," the Attorney General suggested.

"Possibly," the quack nodded.

The pretender volunteered the information that in order to be credible about his new war decoy, he haunted the libraries and book stores to read every book he could borrow or buy about the Spanish conflict and the International Brigades.

"I read so much about the Spanish War that I began to believe that I had fought there, and I knew the fighters and the officers and the Russians whom I read about. I studied the battles, the strategy, and I memorized the names. I talked myself into believing it all."

Questioned in court about his clandestine journeys to East Berlin, Beer was chided, "Were you not afraid to enter a Communist country, knowing that Spanish War veterans were not welcome there?"

"It was known among my friends in East Berlin that I had never fought in Spain," Beer replied, nonplussed.

The trial exposed the nakedness of Beer's disguise. He had not fought in Spain. He never attended the Austrian Military Academy of Wiener-Neustadt. He never belonged to the Vienna "Schutz Bund." He had not earned a Doctor of Philosophy degree in German literature. It was not at all certain that he was Jewish. His life story fell to pieces in the Tel Aviv courtroom. People couldn't believe anything he had said; they concluded that this compulsive liar was not able to tell the truth.

After the trial, he contended that in his one-man crusade to change the direction of Israel foreign policy, he faced a wall of silence. All the newspapers and journals from left to right were closed to him, he charged. During the trial, he was asked, "Did you have the opportunity to publicly express, in speech and in writing, your novel ideas concerning foreign policy?"

"Yes," Beer nodded, "hundreds of times."

"In Israel and abroad?" he was asked.

"Both in Israel and abroad," he replied.

Shortly after the arrest of Israel Beer, the Foreign Ministry declared "Mr. Y" as "persona non grata" and he was requested to leave the country within forty eight hours. His name was never disclosed. The extent of Beer's involvement with "Mr. Y" was brought to light during the court proceedings. Faced with the record compiled by the Security Service of his encounters with the Soviet agent, Beer admitted in court that he met "Mr. Y" dozens of times between 1958 and 1961. He described codes and signs by which they arranged their meetings, in order to mislead any possible detection by counter-espionage agents. One white chalk sign on a wall of a designated building would verify or cancel an appointment.

"Mr. Y" demanded of Beer that he regularly supply information not only of Israel's defense plans and preparations, but also military data of NATO and Western European friends of Israel.

Beer provided "Mr. Y" with secret plans of Zahal, confidential material about national security; lists of Israeli arms purchases in France and West Germany, complete with names of suppliers and intermediate agents; up-to-date information about changes in important Israel Government posts, as well as in the High Command. Beer also furnished "Mr. Y" with data on NATO, particularly its relationships with Israel. Through his trips to Bonn and Berlin, Beer was able to transmit information about West Germany's military developments, and the secret deals between the Adenauer and Ben Gurion regimes.

Capitalizing on the unofficial Israel-France alliance, especially with its close working relationships between the Defense Ministries in Tel Aviv and Paris, Beer never missed a chance on his European trips to visit Paris and renew friendships with high ranking French military and civilian officials.

As a trusted adviser of Ben Gurion and Shimon Peres, Beer was accepted in the Defense establishments in Paris and Bonn, where he could discuss intimate affairs of State and mutual military supply problems. Beer cherished a meeting with Josef Strauss, Adenauer's Minister of Defense. In 1958, he met in Bonn with General Gehlen, Chief of Secret Services.

He had much of value to relay to "Mr. Y" on his return trips to Tel Aviv. Court observers wryly remarked that Tel Aviv was a way station for information from Paris and Bonn.

Beer sought out the friendship of Israeli scientists who worked on research projects for the Ministry of Defense. One night, he recalled, he bumped into "Mr. Y" in the entrance to 67 Brandeis Street.

"What are you doing here?" Beer inquired.

"I've been waiting for you for four hours," was the tired answer. Astounded, Beer wondered what could have induced the Soviet agent to hazard such a risk. "Mr. Y" whispered that he was in a hurry for information about a certain item of scientific research and had to have it in two days.

Disbelieving his lies about his past in Austria and Spain, the Court, however, learned that some of his confessed actions concerning the years of his double duty at the Defense Ministry were substantiated by the investigation. Witnesses verified that certain documents they entrusted to Beer were the ones he said he transferred to "Mr. Y."

The eccentricity of Israel Beer was spotlighted in the

courtroom when he was asked to clear up the contradictions of his "Warsaw Episode."

As the incident unfolded in court, Beer met Gustav Schocken, the editor and publisher of *Haaretz*, soon after his return from a trip to Europe. He confided in the newspaper publisher, who occasionally printed military commentaries by Beer, that on his recent trip he had met a prominent Communist official somewhere in Europe. Beer suggested that *Haaretz* publish an article quoting the Communist personality's advocacy of an eastern approach by Israel in its foreign policy.

"Who was it? Where did you meet? What did he say?" Schocken inquired.

Beer confided that when he visited East Berlin, he went to the Polish Embassy. "I asked for Kummer the Polish Defense Minister in Warsaw, and the call was put through to him. When Kummer spoke to me, he arranged for a special plane to take me to Warsaw. He and I were comrades in arms in Spain. We were together for two days in Warsaw. The Defense Minister of Poland had many important things to say to Israel, and *Haaretz* should give him a chance to say it through me."

Schocken turned down the offer, Beer said.

When Schocken heard about the "Warsaw Episode" he confirmed that Beer told him he had met a key Polish personality in Warsaw, but he never suggested that *Haaretz* publish an article about their talks.

Cross-examined in court about the "Warsaw Episode," Beer admitted: "I was bluffing. I never met the Polish Defense Minister."

"Then why did you tell Mr. Schocken that you did?" pressed the Attorney General.

"I knew that what I told Mr. Schocken of the political orientation of the Warsaw Government was right, but to give greater weight to my arguments and persuade Mr. Schocken to publish the article, I invented the visit to Warsaw," Beer explained.

CHAPTER FOUR

WHO WAS THE REAL BEER?

The Israeli public was still reeling from the shock of the Beer case, and the Supreme Court had just handed down its extended sentence when a new sensation added confusion to a bewildering fantasia.

Out of Switzerland in July 1962, came a new and sickening image of this kaleidoscopic mystery man. The *Schweizer Illustrierte Zeitung* published an article titled "My Friend Beer," written by an English author, Bernard J. Hutton.

"I personally knew Israel Beer when we both lived under the same roof in Moscow during the winter of 1934-35," began the sensational Swiss article.

This introduced an entirely different aspect to the Israel Beer puzzle. Hutton, author of "School of Spies," published dates, places, names. He and Beer lived at the Luks Hotel on Gorki Street in Moscow. It was a Komintern Hotel. They met at the Krasni Mak Cafe. Beer was called "Comrade Kurt."

According to the Hutton article, Beer was born in 1908, not in 1912, and joined the Austrian Communist

Who was the Real Beer?

Party at the age of 20, not the Austrian Social Democratic Party. The young Communist was selected for instruction to be a political teacher and was enrolled in the Party Marxist-Leninist School.

"Comrade Kurt" wrote many articles for Communist publications. Some of his writings were translated for republication in Russian and Czech Party journals. Acquiring a reputation through his writings, he was invited to address Party meetings in many parts of Austria.

Hutton's article claimed that "Comrade Kurt" so distinguished himself in Party work that he earned a scholarship to the Lenin School in Moscow in 1929. After two years of intensive training in Moscow, he was sent back to Vienna in 1931 on a double mission. His task was to serve as a watchman over the "orthodoxy" of the Austrian Communist Party, and also inform Moscow about the internal affairs of the Austrian Party. By 1934, "Comrade Kurt" was Moscow's headman in Austria.

"Comrade Kurt's" reputation in Moscow rose with the effectiveness of his services in Vienna, and he was recalled to the Soviet Capital by Komintern Director Dimitri Zcharievitz Manuilsky for training in the U.S.S.R. Secret Service, the notorious NKVD. It was during this period, November 1934 to January 1935, that Hutton met Beer at the Luks Hotel where they both resided.

Establishing himself in the eyes of NKVD officers as completely trustworthy and qualified, "Comrade Kurt" progressed to advanced training for espionage abroad.

By October 1935, "Comrade Kurt" had passed all tests and had qualified for his assignment as an organizer of spy networks in the West. According to Hutton's story, Beer was sent to Barcelona as an instructor with the International Brigades, serving the Soviet Secret Service. He was ordered to penetrate the Spanish Republican Army General Staff and keep an eye on military operations.

Hutton wrote that Russian generals reported back unfavorably on Beer's military initiatives, and he was recalled to Moscow in December 1936, for disciplinary measures. His conduct in Spain was assailed by NKVD chiefs as "anarchic activity" and he was severely reprimanded and restricted to Moscow. At that time, Hutton encountered Beer again at their favorite cafe and also at the Georgian restaurant, The Moskwa.

"It was painful to see my friend "Comrade Kurt," who usually was so gay and talkative, looking sad and depressed." Hutton wrote. "Kurt hardly spoke to me. He gave the impression that he expected momentarily to be purged. It was the era of the Stalinist purges sweeping the U.S.S.R. "Comrade Kurt" kept a guarded silence, telling me only that he was suffering ill health."

"One day," Hutton wrote, "I bumped into "Comrade Kurt" in the lobby of the Hotel Metropole, Moscow's finest. "Kurt" was his old self again, laughing, happy, a good companion. I asked him: Who is the doctor who cured you? He laughed, A miracle doctor. My health is O.K. again."

Hutton added that he learned later that "Comrade Kurt" had been rehabilitated and rewarded with an honorary membership in the Soviet Military Academy. "Kurt" was sent back to Vienna in February 1937, to direct an espionage network.

In Hutton's magazine article, "Comrade Kurt" was pictured as an excellent servant of the Soviet spy network, relaying to Moscow headquarters accurate, reliable information about the political turmoil in Austria as the Hitlerite Nazis penetrated the body politics while the Austrian Social Democrats fought the reactionary Dollfuss dictatorship and the chaotic nation tottered toward *Anschluss* with Germany.

When Hitler's Panzer columns overran Austria without a fight, "Comrade Kurt" was yanked out of Vienna to be assigned to a safer place, far from the reach of the Communist-hating Nazis.

The NKVD, planning ahead for the Soviet Union's future penetration into the Middle East, trained him for service in Jewish Palestine. He assumed a Jewish identity and background of knowledge of Zionism, Palestine and the Jewish and Arab peoples.

At this point, the story of Beer begins to take the form that was delineated at the trial in the Tel Aviv District Court. The Kurt was dropped for Israel. The Communist experience was watered down to Social Democratic. The Moscow training was omitted from his revised record.

In reviewing the history of Israel "Comrade Kurt" Beer, Hutton analyzed the Soviet spy as a schizophrenic, not in the pathological sense, but as a split person politically and nationally. He rendered signal services to Israel's struggles against the British and the Arabs, applied his creative mind to the elaboration of Israeli military strategy, while on the darker side of his life, he was a pipeline of strategic information to the Soviet Union.

Beer was the traitor par excellence, wrote Hutton, a traitor aware of his treason, a patriot in his own eyes whose military genius was a great asset to Israel, a spy who betrayed Israel to its enemies. Beer was not the first nor the last of the clever spies to penetrate into the ruling circles of host governments.

"One is entitled to wonder," conjectured Hutton, "if a schizophrenic state of mind, a double personality, is not a distinctive sign of Soviet spies faithful to Communism."

Israelis concluded from such personality sketches of Israel Beer, and the testimony published from his trial, that this Judas had only one homeland, not the Jewish State but the Union of Soviet Socialist Republics, to which he gave the last full measure of his devotion.

Hutton's article raised a perplexing question: Who is Beer? Which is the real Beer? What is the truth about the life and treachery of Israel Beer?

Beer was destined to carry the real truth, if there was any truth, to his grave. Only if and when NKVD ever opens its guarded files to outsiders will the truth ever be known, and then perhaps only in the negative. If Hutton's story proved unfounded about a "Comrade Kurt," then the mystery would remain: Did or did not Israel Beer participate in the Spanish Civil War? Did he betray the trust of the Israeli Defense establishment out of a sincere belief that Israel's future security would be better served by an Eastward turn of policy? Or was his treasonable espionage pure and simple a snake-in-the-grass job for the Communists?

What of Beer's actual identity? It became apparent to many followers of the trial that this wolf in sheep's clothing had masqueraded under the name of Israel Beer all these years.

The real Israel Beer, it was widely believed, was a young Jewish student at the University of Berlin who arrived in Vienna in 1938 on his way to Palestine with the aid of the Zionist pioneering youth organization.

Hunted by the Nazis, the Zionist student bore a facial resemblance to the Austrian Communist leader called "Comrade Kurt." This likeness cost the student his life. He disappeared without a trace or a clue. His name, identification papers, and connection with Hechalutz were assumed by "Comrade Kurt" for his NKVD mission to Jewish Palestine.

Beer revealed the disappearance of the Berlin student in his book, but his explanation was that they both struggled to the death for identity papers upon which life itself depended.

Why did Beer admit this murder of an innocent student over possession of identity papers? One plausible theory holds that many Israeli immigrants from Vienna had known an Israel Beer who resided in the Austrian capital during the years that the ex-colonel claimed to have fought in Spain. This line of reasoning contends that the spy had to invent the story of another Israel Beer to support his fabrication of the Spanish War exploits. The disappearance of the other Beer, the student Beer, had to be simulated to explain away the amalgamation of two Beers into one. Incredible? By this time, the Israeli public was in a mood to believe nothing that he said, and to accept anything derogatory against him. The nation felt duped by Mr. Beer.

The authors are inclined to accept the Hutton version of "Comrade Kurt" eliminating the student Beer with the dirty work of the Soviet Secret Service to acquire legitimacy for his NKVD mission to Tel Aviv. We also doubt whether Israel Beer was of Jewish origin. He was not sure of his real identity; this mystery was deepened by Beer's constant refusal to speak of his parents. In retrospect, Hutton's depiction of Beer's Russian Communist training is possible because of his effective espionage for Moscow.

As a young man with education, intelligence and an affinity for the intellectual socialist circles dominated by Jewish leftists, Beer undoubtedly had many Jewish friends and connections in Vienna. His familiarity with Jews, his reading of Herzl's *Judenstadt,* his natural interest in Palestine in this Viennese center of Zionism, qualified him as a natural candidate for NKVD service in the ancient homeland of the Jews.

From the viewpoint of the Komintern in the Kremlin, there were long-term and short-term goals for their underground operatives in the Palestine area. Moscow required information and organization in the Middle East which had been a goal of imperialist expansion both in Czarist and Stalinist days. The Soviets also regarded the growing Jewish community in Palestine as a fertile field for Communist Party organization.

Who was the Real Beer?

Communist ideologists always looked upon the Russian Zionists as reactionary nationalists who could not be trusted in the Soviet Union. Persecuted in the U.S.S.R., Zionists fled to Palestine and other havens and were regarded by the Communists as enemies of the Soviet Union. Yet, in Palestine, Moscow nurtured a small Communist Party as an agent provocateur to the authorities.

Beer's initial contacts in Jewish Palestine were not with the Communists, who never succeeded in gaining more than a tiny fraction of public support. He chose instead to align himself with the ruling party, Mapai Labor, led by Ben Gurion, as a pragmatic vehicle for burrowing into the establishment.

This was the most practical avenue for gaining access to high places, in the military as well as in the civilian administration.

Under investigation, Beer admitted that he did not make his first contacts with Soviet agents until the middle 1950's. This meant a delay of fifteen years before he could produce results for Moscow. But it was a decade and a half worth waiting for, because he utilized the time to cultivate the right people and build up his reputation and position for maximum double dealing and chicanery.

The major question aroused by the Beer case was how much damage did he cause the State of Israel by being a conduit of defense and strategic information for Moscow?

Did he tip off the enemy, through their suppliers in Russia, about the plans for the 1956 Sinai War? How much vital data was transmitted to Moscow concerning the secret Tel Aviv-Paris transactions? What information, if any, from Beer enabled the Kremlin to pull off its colossal bluff threatening to fire nuclear rockets if the Israel-British-French Sinai-Suez invasion of Egypt were not stopped? It was learned after the Sinai War that President Bulganin was faking; the Kremlin had no intentions of resorting to atomic warfare. It was learned however that the Soviet leadership had been reliably informed that only the threat of nuclear attack could stop the British and French from recapturing the Suez Canal: Beer knew how much Ben Gurion feared Soviet intervention.

Beer's frequent trips to Europe and his talks with top level French and other European leaders probably enabled him to advise the Kremlin about the reaction that could be expected in Paris, London and Jerusalem in the face of threatened Soviet military intervention to save Egypt.

When the Israel Supreme Court raised the question of whether Beer had endangered the security of Israel, or committed irreparable damage, the judges' distinction reflected the assumption of many of the nation's leaders — Beer had sold out many vital secrets to Moscow, and through the Soviets to their Egyptian clients.

CHAPTER FIVE

A TUNNEL UNDER THE EMBASSY

Whatever the opinion of specialists concerning the Beer case, it clearly indicates how eager the Soviet Union has been to introduce its agents in the top political circles of the Jewish State. Obviously, the fact that Beer failed, and that an important official of the U.S.S.R. Embassy in Tel Aviv hurriedly departed from Israel, by no means put an end to the activities of Soviet Secret Service in the country.

Indeed, it was only after Beer had died that the Kremlin leaders planned an operation with no precedent in the history of international espionage, in order to gain access to the secrets of the State of Israel. A kind of underground tunnel was dug through the administrative heart of Moscow which led to the Israeli Embassy from the foundations of an adjoining building. This tunnel was to provide Soviet leaders with permanent access to the Embassy building, and allow them to have installed, only a few yards from the Ambassador's desk, the most sophisticated electronic devices. When, in the fall of 1965, the tunnel was discovered by members of the Embassy staff, this almost led to a diplomatic scandal. But Israel decided to hush up the affair, so as to spare the Soviet Union public embarassment.

The authors of this work, having talked to a number of foreign diplomats posted in Paris, Brussels, and Stockholm, but who had served in Moscow at the time the affair of the tunnel broke out, were thus enabled to reconstitute the case in its general outline, such as it is described here.

Long before 1965, the Americans had found out that a transmitting and receiving post had been installed by the Soviet Secret Service behind the wrought-iron eagle which decorated a wall in one of the conference rooms of the United States Embassy in Moscow. It had long been common knowledge that the Soviets constantly watched all foreign embassies, and listened in on all the conversations that took place. Nevertheless, professional diplomats considered it as an impertinence exceeding all bounds to hide a microphone behind the eagle emblem of the United States. The Kremlin was to do better still, and to demonstrate that where espionage is concerned it is prepared to spend lavishly and forget about good manners.

Since 1948, the Israeli Embassy had occupied a small building not far from the imposing structure housing the Soviet Union's Ministry of Foreign Affairs. The building had become too small to accommodate services which had considerably expanded over a period of fifteen years. The Israeli Embassy requested from the Soviet Government authorization to purchase a larger building. The appropriate Soviet authorities offered to build a new chancery for a lump sum, rather than provide a building already in existence. Israel was agreeable to this proposal, a plot in the center of Moscow was selected, and the building was erected according to the design of an Israeli architect. The building was so planned that it would also serve as the residence of the Ambassador and of some of his collaborators. The Israeli Embassy soon moved to its new premises.

Embassy employees were arranging furniture on the ground floor when they noticed that one square of the waxed parquet floor gave off a hollow sound, as if it covered an empty space. They removed the flooring and discovered a dark hole which gradually widened into a tunnel large enough for two men to stand in with ease. The two employees entered the hole, discovered a passageway at the bottom, four to five yards beneath the Embassy building, and were able to move forward for about thirty yards. They finally reached an exit which was blocked by an iron gate. This gave way under their pressure, and as the employees came up, they were astounded to find themselves in the courtyard of the building adjoining the Embassy which, at ground level, was separated from it by a high wall. The two employees immediately retraced their steps, returning to the Embassy through the tunnel, while carefully avoiding a third passage they came across. They burst in to tell the Ambassador about their unexpected discovery.

Thus, the building which the Soviet authorities had built to house the Israeli Embassy was so contrived as to give Soviet agents direct inner access to it. The head of Israel's delegation was still pondering what steps to take, when the tunnel was suddenly flooded. The water had almost reached the ground floor when an anonymous telephone call gave warning that a water pipe had just burst in the adjoining courtyard, and that all necessary precautions should be taken to prevent the building from being flooded.

In all probability, observers posted in the building next to the Embassy had seen the Israelis exploring the secret tunnel. The Soviet Secret Service, giving way to panic, had attempted to erase all traces of their industry by flooding the tunnel.

The Six Day War broke out over a year after the tunnel affair. The Soviet Union, having brought the Arab countries to stumble into war and their ensuing defeat, thereupon broke off diplomatic relations with Israel. Even then, Israel did not divulge the affair of the tunnel. The foreign diplomats with whom the authors discussed the matter wondered whether the Israeli Government had been right at the time, to do no more than address a discreet protest to Moscow through the intermediary of Mr. Zubakhin, the Soviet Union's Ambassador to Israel. The main argument used to justify this moderation is that in any case the tunnel had been rendered useless by the very fact of its discovery. Under the circumstances, Israel had acted wisely, all the more so since it could not possibly foresee that its diplomatic relations with the Soviet Union would soon come to an end.

Viewed from a certain angle, the affair of the tunnel

emphasizes the vital importance the Soviet Union attributes to a state as small as Israel. The Soviet Union's interest in Israel derives from a number of sources, most of which have already been described in the chapter dealing with Israel Beer. Suffice it to add that Israel, inasmuch as it is the homeland of the Jewish people, feels strong affinities with the three million Jews still living in the Soviet Union, and, on the other hand, maintains close bonds with the influential American Jewish community. Furthermore, it enjoys good relations with the Western world, and this gives it, in the eyes of Moscow, the character of an "imperialist base." For Moscow, Israel was, and still is, a strategic springboard from which it is easy, under certain conditions of which Soviet Intelligence is perfectly aware, to penetrate into a number of political and military circles in Western Europe. Thus, Moscow has never hesitated to use Israel for espionage maneuvers and operations whose final objectives are at times far removed from Jerusalem. As in the case of Beer, the U.S.S.R. has frequently taken advantage of the fact that on the basis of the Law of Return, any Jew, of whatever country of origin, is entitled to settle in Israel, if he expresses the wish to do so.

At one time, the Soviet Union granted permission to a few hundred Soviet Jews to emigrate to Israel, in spite of the fact that Zionism as such was banned within the boundaries of the Soviet Republics. In most cases, the Soviet Union justified these exceptions to its general policy on humanitarian grounds, such as the reunion of families separated as the result of the war. Nothing was easier for the Soviet Union than to slip one of its agents among bona fide immigrant. Its services could also recruit authentic Soviet Jews who were prepared to spy in Israel. There existed even simpler ways to send Secret Service agents to Israel. Jewish emigration, severely restricted in the Soviet Union proper, was, for a number of years, open to practically all Jews in many satellite countries, such as Poland, Hungary, Bulgaria, Czechoslovakia and Rumania. Since the Intelligence Services of these countries operate in close collaboration with, or under the direct control of the Soviet G.R.U. Intelligence apparatus, it was even easier to slip in dozens of spies among the thousands of Jewish emigrants coming from Poland and Rumania. Dramatic cases have come to light about Jewish immigrants who were compelled to spy in Israel for some Eastern European Secret Service, under the threat that their close relatives who had stayed behind would have a rough time of it, should the agent fail to obey his instructions to the letter. In other words, the family that remained in a Communist country was at the mercy of the Secret Service. The new immigrant, who had, often unwillingly, become a Soviet agent, was neatly trapped, unless he was prepared to see his aged parents, a brother or sister, and in some cases, even his own children, sacrificed.

Public opinion in Israel was aroused when it learned about one such case, through the verdict of the Jerusalem Court which judged a spy from Eastern Europe on January 19, 1965.

The accused, a Jewish immigrant, was condemned

for espionage on behalf of a Communist country. For safety's sake, the Court, in passing judgment, did not divulge the name of the accused nor his country of origin. We quote an excerpt of the judgment : "The judges have taken into consideration the fact that when he reached Israel the accused was subjected to cruel pressure on the part of the foreign agent who manipulated him. But they have also been in a position to ascertain that the accused voluntarily threw himself under the wolf's claws in his country of birth before emigrating to Israel. That he did not address himself to Israel's Security Services for aid and protection obviously aggravates his case."

The new immigrant, who had remained in close touch with the foreign agent manipulating him, was uncovered by Israeli counter-espionage two years after he had settled in Israel. He was condemned to a seven-year prison sentence. In his country of origin, in Eastern Europe, he had been thoroughly trained, and his implantation in Israel had been carefully planned. He had been told to settle in Israel, find work there, adapt himself to the conditions prevailing in the country, and to widen his circle of acquaintances in a well defined milieu. Only when he had fulfilled these initial conditions did his manipulator order him to transmit information.

The activities of Soviet agents in Israel inevitably aroused the interest of neighboring Arab countries. Egypt in particular, concomitant with the military and economic aid provided by the Soviet Union, wished to obtain worthwhile information data gathered directly in Israel. On more than one occasion, the Soviet Union took advantage of this state of affairs to arouse the U.A.R. and other Arab countries by transmitting erroneous information about Israel. Let us recall that the information Moscow forwarded to Damascus, concerning an "imminent Israeli attack against Syria," was, as has already been indicated, the direct cause of the Six Day War.

Mr. Zubakhin, the U.S.S.R. Ambassador to Israel, and a former intelligence officer in Eastern Africa, personally directed the operations of Soviet agents. Enjoying diplomatic immunity and a privileged social position, the Soviet Ambassador could move freely throughout Israel's territory, and meet whomever he pleased.

Knowing they were constantly watched by Israeli counter-espionage, the Soviets made use of the less vulnerable embassies of their satellites. The Rumanian Embassy, up to the crisis in Rumanian-Soviet relations, and, somewhat later, the Polish Embassy were, from 1960 onward, the real centers of Soviet espionage in Israel—which does not mean that other embassies, the Czech one, for instance, were not also active in this field. But the Polish and Rumanian diplomats could operate more easily, owing to the fact that they were on friendly terms with many people among the large number of new settlers born in Poland or Rumania. This type of settler therefore attracted the special attention of the G.R.U. But, up to his departure in 1967, the unseen power, the leader among spies operating in Israel, was Mr. Zubakhin himself.

An amusing episode in the secret war Eastern European countries conducted under Soviet guidance throws light on some of their methods. The unwitting hero of this story was an Israeli diplomat visiting Poland. As soon as he had settled down in his room in one of the fine hotels of the Polish capital, the diplomat went to his bathroom to take a shower. At the very moment when, stark naked, he got under the steaming shower, a young Polish woman burst into the bathroom, and with no further ado offered her charms. Once the shock of surprise had passed, the Israeli wrapped himself in a bath towel, and, politely requesting the young woman to leave, warned her, "otherwise, I shall have to complain to the hotel management." He did not want to say "the Director of Intelligence Services," although he knew full well, as did all Western diplomats posted in Eastern Europe, that the female charmer is a classical bait, her role consisting of placing the foreign diplomat in a situation so embarrassing that he can hardly fail to collaborate with the Secret Service. Certain pictures, taken at the opportune moment, have often proved highly effective in blackmailing the unfortunate victims.

We shall mention one last episode of this secret war, one which hit the front pages of the Western press soon after the Six Day War. Ambassador Zubakhin had already returned to Moscow where, probably on account of the failure of his intelligence network in Israel to predict accurately the rapid military collapse of the Arabs, he was kept away from all public functions. Since, with the exception of Rumania, all the Communist countries had broken off relations with Israel, only "planted" agents remained in the country.

It was at this time—August 1967—when the Czech spring had not yet blossomed, that Mr. Charles Jordan, an American citizen and President of the American Joint, reached Prague. He wished to gather information on the precarious situation of Jews in Communist countries following the Six Day War. He registered at the Esplanade Hotel, one reserved for foreign tourists, and got in touch with the local authorities in order to organize the ceremonies that would commemorate the first millenary of the Jewish community of Prague where the famous Golem came into being. Toward evening, on the second day of their sojourn, Mr. Jordan told his wife that he was going out to get a newspaper. He vanished — never to return. Thirty-six hours later, his body was found floating on the Vitava (Moldau) river in the center of Prague.

The Prague authorities declared to the U.S. Ambassador that Jordan's death was the result of drowning. The American Ambassador had a hard time obtaining authorization that the body be examined by Swiss doctors, who were urgently called in from Geneva. Prague, at the time, was still under the thumb of the Stalinist Novotny.

Clearly, Jordan had not gone to Prague in order to commit suicide. His death was probably due to the fact that, in Israel, he had attended the conference of Jewish "millionaires" who had rushed to support Israel, and he was thus in possession of information on economic and social matters that could be of interest to Eastern-European and Arab countries. In any case the JOINT, which distributed various kinds of aid to Jewish refugees from Eastern Europe, had long been considered by Moscow as "an organ of international Jewry and American imperialism." From there to the murder of Jordan only one step needed to be taken. It remains to be discovered who was interested in having Jordan assassinated and for what purpose.

This mystery has not yet been elucidated. More might have been discovered had the Czech spring not been nipped in the bud. Some theories were put forward by Washington, others by Israeli authorities, but they all remain mere suppositions.

Charles Jordan was kidnapped as he left his hotel by one of the special services of a Soviet satellite, in the hope of extracting information from him that was hard to come by since the satellite countries no longer had embassies functioning in Israel. He may have been intimidated and tortured by his kidnappers, and been mortally wounded as he tried to defend himself. In order to prevent an international scandal from breaking out, and to blur their tracks, his attackers then staged a faked suicide, and threw his body into the river, only to "discover" it later.

According to another version, spread in Vienna by "well-informed" Communist agents, it was neither Soviet nor Czech services which had kidnapped and murdered Jordan, but an "Egyptian Commando" then undergoing training in a specialized school near Prague. But this version looks like a red herring intended as a diversion, rather than a true account of this sinister affair.

In Prague, during the summer of 1968, the Red Army

prevented the disclosure of certain atrocities committed during the Stalin era by Czech and other services working in close collaboration with or under the direction of the Kremlin's Secret Service. Obviously, in Prague, more than one intelligence officer knows the truth concerning Charles Jordan's death. But before it can be known who threw Jordan's body into the Vitava, a great deal of water will flow through that river.

PART II

SHADOWS OVER THE PYRAMIDS

CHAPTER SIX

ISRAEL'S "EYE IN CAIRO"

On a wet and wintry February night in 1968, a disparate trio stood apart from other passengers waiting in the cavernous departure hall of Cairo-West Airport. Under the glare of neon lights, one of the three, a robust, handsome man, seemed pale and worn. He gripped the hand of his companion, an attractive youthful blonde. They conversed in subdued tones with a black-cassocked Catholic priest.

Standing nearby, four men in mufti kept their eyes glued on the couple and on the cleric. The four inspectors of the United Arab Republic State Security Service were there to ascertain that the couple did not miss their flight, that would whisk them far away from Egypt.

At three a.m., the sleepy travelers slouching in their armchairs were aroused by the loudspeaker blaring: "Passengers on Lufthansa Flight 674 to Athens and Munich are requested to present themselves, with their tickets, at exit gate three."

Father Unkrieg, spiritual leader of the German Catholic community in Cairo, barely had time to mutter, "please give my regards to my friends in Munich," when the four inspectors closed in on the man and woman and led them straight to the gangway of the German airline's Boeing 707. The chief inspector removed two passports from his inside pocket and wordlessly handed them to the couple.

When the Boeing landed in Munich on the morning of February 4, the man and his blonde companion were not on board. Newspaper reporters who had been tipped to the scheduled arrival of the mystery couple returned to their newsrooms empty-handed. They learned later that the long-awaited couple had "vanished" en route.

The man, who dozed through the flight, and his wife, left the plane in Athens, taking their meager luggage. Two men greeted them at the Greek airport, exchanged their flight tickets, put them on another plane an hour later, destination London.

On February 6, while Munich reporters speculated as to the couple's disappearance, the pair landed at Lod Airport, near Tel Aviv, smiling, and dressed in new clothes bought during a day's stop-over in London.

Thus ended the odyssey of a remarkable man nick-named, "Our Eye in Cairo," the Israeli spy, Wolfgang Lotz, condemned in 1965 to life imprisonment by an Egyptian Court. His release from jail had been neither a miracle, nor an act of clemency by President Gamal Abdul Nasser. "Our Eye" and his wife were released in exchange for nine Egyptian generals captured in Israel's lightning sweep through Sinai, during the Six Day War of 1967.

Israel's "Eye in Cairo"

Why was it necessary for the spy, whom the Egyptian police had released and seen off on a flight to Athens, to vanish at Athens Airport? Why did the Israelis resort to this sleight of hand? No sooner had this master spy won his release from Egyptian captivity than he ran the risk of standing trial again in a West German Federal Court on a charge of usurping his German citizenship.

That is why Frau Waltraud Lotz could not telephone her parents, who lived in Heilbronn, Germany, either from Athens or London, to break the happy news of her liberation at her husband's side. This oversight caused Mrs. Klara Noumann, Waltraud's aged mother, to comment that "She might at least have called up to say hello after all these years." Mrs. Noumann did not know that her son-in-law Wolfgang Lotz was one of the greatest spies of our time.

The "official" story of Wolfgang Lotz, "Israel's Eye in Cairo"—as unfolded before the Supreme Court of State Security in Egypt on June 28, 1965, begins in West Berlin on a summer day in 1960. According to the evidence led in Cairo, the opening scene took place in a riding club where the German citizen, Wolfgang Lotz, recently had been engaged as an equestrian master.

Solidly built, walking with a horseman's gait, red-haired, his bright green eyes flashing, Lotz, who was born in Mannheim in 1921, and baptized Johann Sigmund Wolfgang, was reared for horsemanship. His father had been "Rittmeister" (riding master) under the old regime. Wolfgang inherited from his father a love of horses.

During the Second World War, Wolfgang served as

an army officer under General Rommel's command in North Africa. In the Libyan desert, Lotz came to know and appreciate Arabian racing steeds. After the war, he worked in turn as a truck driver in Australia, a stable boy, a coach, a trainer and as riding master in West Berlin.

On that summer day in 1960, he met another horse lover, who introduced himself as Elias Gordon. They naturally talked about horses, and at Gordon's invitation, had drinks at the riding club's bar.

Suddenly, Elias Gordon, who spoke German fluently, but with an indefinable accent—either Slavic or Arabic— surprised Lotz with an astounding offer. Leaning towards Lotz and lowering his voice, Gordon inquired, "What would you say about your managing a stable of thoroughbreds?"

How else could an equine-devotee react? "It is my fondest dream," Lotz replied enthusiastically, spontaneously, imprudently. Much later, he would come to realize the extent of his impetuousity. Then it was too late. Without being aware of it, then and there at the club bar, Lotz was caught in the web where a secret agent is recruited by the Intelligence Services of a foreign country.

"I shall introduce you to a rich and influential friend of mine as soon as you wish. He is looking for someone capable of managing a stable of thoroughbreds." Gordon went on. "I'm convinced he'll like you, and I think the deal is in the bag. Of course, it's all up to you."

An appointment was made with the "rich and influential friend," whom Gordon carefully refrained from identifying by name. Lotz was to know that name before the week was out. They met in a luxurious West Berlin restaurant. Lotz was caught in a cross fire between Gordon, always friendly and persuasive, and his wealthy friend, who acted reassuring and understanding, and who told Lotz his name in a barely audible whisper—Rudy Bernstein.

"Rudy, of that I'm sure. But about the name Bernstein, I'm not certain... We were soon on the friendliest terms. I called him Rudy. He simply called me Lotz. It was customary in Berlin for my friends to call me by my family name. But when all is taken into account, I do think his name was Bernstein," Wolfgang Lotz testified in June 1965, before the Supreme Court of State Security in Cairo.

Lotz was sorely tempted by the offer proposed by Rudy Bernstein, whom he later described as elegant, grey-haired, suave, scented by fine cologne.

Rudy Bernstein explained, "For some time now, I've been longing to acquire a fine stable of thoroughbreds in Egypt. I have the means to do it, but unfortunately, only at a distance. Too many business interests hold me down in Germany."

He added, in a detached tone, with an expression of complete trust in Elias Gordon. "Elias knows you well. He watched you around your stable long before he approached you. He is convinced you are the man I need. So—well I've made my offer. It's up to you to decide whether you accept it, and what would be your terms. I'm prepared to listen."

91

The story is almost as old as mankind. Lotz, a riding master without a care in the world fell for flattery. Fascinated by the vision of his dream coming true, he surrendered his freedom that moment when he agreed to go to Egypt and see the prospects for himself. Rudy Bernstein had caught his fish in his carefully-laid net.

During the fall of 1960, Lotz met Elias Gordon many times. They studied the problems of horse breeding in Egypt and figured out costs and other particulars which Gordon promised to submit to his friend Rudy.

In January 1961, Wolfgang Lotz made his first trip to Cairo, checking into a small, modest hotel, "El Zahara," in the heart of the city. Elias Gordon advanced money for six weeks in Egypt, to study the possibilities of opening a riding school and acquiring a small breeding stable, with six horses.

For the first time in his life, Lotz enjoyed a life of luxury and independence. No one in Cairo held him to account. He had found what he wanted. On his return to Europe, Lotz presented an enthusiastic account of his Cairo prospects to Rudy Bernstein when they met in Munich, as always in the company of Elias Gordon. This meeting, late in February 1961, represented the crucial moment that Western Intelligence Services call the "I.S. approach":* "This phase sometimes occurs quite some time after the previous phase, that of initial contact."

The "dealer," intimately knew the personality of Lotz.

---

* "On Espionage and Good Manners," Defense et Sécurité du Territoire, Paris, 1968.

Now came the time to utilize those character traits which appear most promising: love of money, ideological affinities, personal weaknesses, role-playing, professional ambition. The dealer, once sure of his subject, risks his first request for information, a harmless bid which seems so natural because it calls upon the subject to talk about familiar matters which he knows at first hand. The purpose of his initial request for information is to test the subject's reactions.

The ultimate phase, actual recruitment, promptly followed. In Lotz's case it developed faster than expected.

Rudy Bernstein met Lotz again the following day—this time without Gordon. Lotz was enthusiastic about the island of Gezirah, up the river from Cairo. Gezirah was the meeting place of Egypt's military brass and Cairo's horse-riding elite. It was at Gezirah's smart, exclusive hippodrome that Lotz established his first friendships in Cairo.

Rudy appeared to be more interested in the Egyptian officers and German technicians who congregated there, and in former Nazis occasionally seen at Gezirah. He prodded Lotz. Yes, at Gezirah, he had seen generals, colonels, and other important people whose names and functions he did not know. Yes, he heard German spoken by people whom the Egyptians treated with respect and deference.

"We shall need a great many more details in this respect," Rudy remarked casually. Changing the subject abruptly, he informed Lotz, "Your permanent settlement in Egypt does not depend on me alone. A friend to whom

I shall introduce you will make the necessary arrangements."

Lotz was perplexed. Still, he refrained from asking questions, fearful that his dream of running his own breeding stable might evaporate. He had enjoyed his first visit to Egypt, wanted to return there and was prepared to pay the price.

He therefore met Rudy's friend upon whom his Cairo venture depended. Lotz already grasped that he would not get something for nothing.

"Mr. Joseph," the mystery man, bore no resemblance to Rudy Bernstein and Elias Gordon. They played roles that fitted them like gloves. Rudy, the born millionaire, who didn't know what to do with his money; Gordon, the man who loved horses and lived high above his income, thanks to the generosity of Rudy. "Mr. Joseph" —Lotz would never know his real name—was of a different breed. He should have every reason to cover up his game. Paradoxically he hid nothing.

"I am the head of Israel's Intelligence in Europe," Mr. Joseph declared. "Rudy is our permanent representative in West Germany, Gordon is our man in West Berlin."

Lotz was astounded. Finding himself face-to-face with professional spies flabbergasted him. The realization that he, a former officer of the Wehrmacht, should be confronting Israelis—Jews—was nothing less than fantastic.

What really tipped the scales as Lotz decided to become Israel's secret agent in Cairo? The lure of breeding horses? Or the fear of this ex-Nazi officer of Jews who stopped at nothing? In 1965, in the Cairo Court, Lotz's lawyer dwelt on "the German collective complex" towards the "Jewish people." The court judged that, under the circumstances, this argument constituted a plausible motivation.

"Mr. Joseph," one of the chiefs of Israel Intelligence, had gone to Munich specifically to make a deal with Lotz. "Mr. Joseph" impressed Lotz with his direct approach. Tall, slender, his head crowned with a mop of unruly hair, his German poor, interspersed with Yiddish, "Joseph" went straight to the point: "You will have your riding school and breed your horses, Mr. Lotz. You'll get everything you need. But you will have to be of service to us."

"Fine, Mr. Joseph. I'll do whatever you wish," Lotz promised.

Did he understand that this meant supplying Israel with information about Egypt?

Certainly. But he imagined, mistakenly, that all he would need to do was to glean bits of gossip here and there, once he settled down in Cairo. He did not suspect that espionage is a tough profession, demanding painstaking training.

The apprenticeship of Israel's future spy in the U.A.R. started in March 1961, after Lotz's trip to West Berlin to wind up his affairs and say farewell to his friends, telling them he would settle in Cairo. He returned to Munich where "Mr. Joseph" rented a bachelor's studio for him. This was on a quiet side street. His instructors were four specialists of Israel's Secret Service,

95

who had come from Tel Aviv to train the new recruit. Under strict supervision of "Mr. Joseph," they alternated in teaching him, eight hours a day, the skills and tricks of his new profession: transmitting and receiving radio messages, coding and decoding, using invisible ink for dispatching secret information, preparing invisible ink from simple materials, microfilming documents, discreetly photographing notables, military installations and strategic positions, using light arms and explosives.

During this intensive training (from March to September 1961), Lotz was paid a monthly salary of $ 250, plus expenses. While the Tel Aviv technicians were training the muscular red-headed Lotz, who was better at taming wild horses than manipulating delicate instruments, "Mr. Joseph" lectured him in a crash course on the geo-politics of the Middle East.

The spy student knew little about the country employing him, but he learned much about Nasser and his government, political divisions within Egypt, the civilian establishment, the organization of the army, the top men in the regime and their opponents, the structure of the Egyptian police and the character of the U.A.R. Intelligence Services.

Over and over again "Mr. Joseph" drilled it into Lotz that everything about Egypt's ruling circles was of interest to Israel. Any information concerning changes in political orientation, personnel, make-up or structure within the ministries and armed forces, must be transmitted immediately to Tel Aviv. This was the task for which he would be supplied with funds for the purchase and operation of his "plaything"—as "Mr. Joseph" called the equine establishment.

"Supply us with precise, detailed information. Accuracy and speed are essential to the success of your mission," "Mr. Joseph" reiterated. Lotz gradually became fascinated with his espionage training. He previously had known only what he read in spy novels and saw in thriller films.

Besides theory which he lectured Lotz three to four hours weekly, "Mr. Joseph" directed his student to throw lavish parties for officers and socialites who would become habitués of the riding school.

"Remember that the smart, horse-riding, race-going set belongs mostly to the old aristocracy and upper middle class. They feel more attached to the old monarchy than to Nasser's socialist ideas. These officers and notables, while formally voicing allegiance to Nasser, constantly plot to overthrow him. You shall spot them with ease. They speak mockingly of Nasser and his regime. They are seldom to be taken seriously. They undermine decisions taken at the highest political level, while living off public funds. When they sign checks for their riding lessons, know that a road should have been built with that money.

"Still, it's possible," Joseph continued, "that some day there will be a real attempt to do away with Nasser. These corrupt officers and notables might conceivably draw into such a plot an important member of Nasser's immediate entourage. That's the sort of thing you should find out about before it actually happens, and warn us in time. You'll be able to distinguish soon enough between the empty boasting of Cairo's high society and a realistic, well-planned operation which would bring about a radically new situation."

"Supposing I could give you such advance warning, what would you do with that information?" Lotz inquired innocently.

"It is not and it will never be your role to ask questions. We ask the questions. We interpret the answers. You are going to Cairo to answer, as best you can, the questions Tel Aviv will ask you. Remember that. It will spare us further misunderstandings."

Wolfgang Lotz had little leisure time, so busy was he training to become Israel's spy in Egypt. He went to the cinema occasionally, and enjoyed having a beer in a Munich beer hall alone or in the company of one of his instructors. One evening, Lotz met a young woman, Waltraud Martha Noumann. A buxom blonde just turned thirty, she lived alone in Munich. A few weeks after they met she declared herself willing to link her life with Wolfgang Lotz. She was willing to go with him to Egypt.

"Mr. Joseph" was unenthusiastic when he learned that Lotz wanted to take his blonde to Cairo. A quick, discreet inquiry revealed the past of Waltraud Noumann. Born in 1931 in East Germany, she had been employed as a maid from 1945 to 1947 by a high party official in East Germany. In 1947, she crossed over to West Germany with her family. Her parents settled in Stuttgart, where they opened a modest shop selling brushes. Waltraud worked as maid or children's nurse in various homes. In 1956, she emigrated to the United States, as an "au pair" maid. Shortly after her return from the United States to Munich, she met and fell in love with Lotz. "Mr. Joseph" tried to talk Lotz out of taking Waltraud.

"I won't go without Waltraud. I'm willing to do all you ask of me, but it is out of the question for me to go alone," Lotz informed "Mr. Joseph."

In July 1961 Lotz sailed on an Italian liner to Alexandria, with Waltraud at his side. They were not married, so Lotz introduced Waltraud as his fiancee. They shipped a Volkswagen. Among the half dozen pairs of boots that Lotz packed in his suitcases, one hid in a double heel a miniaturized radio transmitter and receiver, made in Israel. Waltraud knew nothing about her lover's secret mission.

Lotz was to receive a monthly salary of $ 850, in addition to $ 1500 a month's operating fund for the horse-breeding enterprise. The money was deposited with the Cairo branch of a German bank.

As soon as they arrived in Cairo, the couple rented a luxurious villa in the old city center. They lived on a grand scale. The modest riding master from West Berlin suddenly was posing as a wealthy breeder of horses. His parties at the finest restaurants had French champagne and Scotch whiskey flowing freely. He rapidly cultivated many good friends among the racing fans at Cairo's hippodrome. Being knowledgeable about race horses, his advice was sought and valued. Lotz bought five thoroughbreds for $ 4500 and rented a stable in Gezirah, near the

Pyramids. His professional competence and high living attracted clients among the Cairene elite who revolve around the hippodrome and polo fields of Gezirah. He rubbed shoulders with high Egyptian officers who shared his fondness for horses. Lotz entertained members of Cairo's German colony, including the technicians and engineers employed by Egypt to develop ground-to-ground missiles which Nasser had ordered. Lotz established a solid friendship with the Kiesows—Frantz, the agent in Egypt of the German steel-producing firm, "Mannesmann," and his Egyptian-born wife, Nadia.

Within four months, Lotz felt solidly established in Cairo, successfully exploiting his small breeding stable, and starting to prove his gratitude to his sponsors, "Mr. Joseph," Rudy Bernstein and Elias Gordon.

In December 1961, "Mr. Joseph" called Lotz for a first working report to be delivered personally.

Leaving Waltraud in Cairo, Lotz flew to Munich where Rudy enjoined him to proceed to Paris. "Mr. Joseph" awaited Lotz in a cafe near the Etoile, on December 22, 1961. Around five p.m. Lotz, reporting his "penetration" in Cairo, spoke effusively of his newly established wide circle of friends and acquaintances in the Egyptian capital. "Mr. Joseph" expressed his satisfaction and judged it was time for his agent to become operative. After they cheerily celebrated Christmas in Paris night clubs, Lotz returned to Cairo. He started operating his tiny transmission set. He transmitted two or three times weekly to Tel Aviv on a specified wave-length. The first code he learned was very simple, to ease his task and also to lead astray Egyptian counter espionage. 001 stands for A, 002 for B, 003 for C, and so on to Z. The incredible amateurishness of this code dislocated the vigilant Egyptian counter-intelligence.

Convinced that Lotz was capable of supplying valuable information, "Mr. Joseph" encouraged him by raising his monthly salary, from $ 850 to $ 1050 starting January 1962. "Mr. Joseph" also handed Lotz a $ 10,000 check for the purchase of a large villa on the banks of the Nile. Lotz's standard of living climbed higher. Waltraud and Wolfgang happily emulated the lush life of wealthy owners of thoroughbreds.

Until July 1962, all went well in Cairo, much to the satisfaction of Israeli Intelligence. Lotz rented his horses to government and military VIP's, and gave riding lessons, even to officers of the mounted police. Many clients became close friends, and they developed mutual trust.

Lotz invited his friends to his luxurious home, where Waltraud welcomed them warmly and entertained royally. The Kiesows were frequent guests. From party to party, the Lotz home atmosphere became cosier and more intimate. Lotz invited beautiful young women of doubtful virtue to his parties. The guests chatted freely, uninhibited, late into the night, drinking unstintingly. The guest rooms in the spacious Lotz villa were open, particularly to army officers and their newly-acquired girlfriends. Out of their romantic conversations, Lotz gained information for two or three transmissions a week. Colonel Ahmed, who took riding lessons regularly, suddenly cancelled his appointment for the following week, because he was assigned to the Suez Canal zone "for important maneuvers." The information was immediately transmitted to Tel Aviv. A high official knew more than the newspapers reported about Nasser's meeting with the ambassador of a Western Power. The smart set at Gezirah's hippodrome talked of troop movements in the Sinai peninsula. Tel Aviv received this information from Lotz. Checking Lotz's news items against other sources, Tel Aviv ascertained Lotz's credibility. A neophyte in the profession, his information was seldom of crucial importance, but it was always exact, reliable and consequently extremely valuable to the military and political Intelligence of the Jewish State.

Lotz's informers were unsuspecting collaborators. None of them harbored any suspicion of conspiracy towards this strapping, good-natured Germanic type, who often recalled with fond nostalgia "his" desert experiences in General Rommel's Afrika Korps. At the Lotz parties, a guest could meet Colonel Hadini, chief of Cairo's mounted police, a devoted horse fan, who openly displayed his admiration for Wolfgang and Waltraud. Another frequent guest was Mr. El Zaher, Minister of Agriculture, a colorless potentate. By a chance encounter at Gezirah, the Minister became a permanent fixture in the Lotz home, unwittingly supplying first hand information of Cabinet deliberations and farm problems. Wolfgang Lotz was delighted to extend his genial hospitality to the esteemed vice-president of the Council of Ministers, a close confidant of President Nasser, Mr. El Shafai. A talkative bon vivant after savoring the fine western-style cuisine of Waltraud's cook, El Shafai was a rich lode which Wolfgang diligently mined for long coded messages to Tel Aviv.

Lotz's closest confidant was General Yussef Gahurib, governor of a military zone. Lotz's fraternity included the entourage of ex-King Farouk. At this juncture of U.A.R. history, remnants of the Royal Court still enjoyed Nasser's tolerance. They were hail fellows well met, while drinking Lotz's whiskey with officials of the regime which toppled Farouk.

Much as he enjoyed the conviviality of his Egyptian fellowship, Lotz appreciated and sought out another German who had been living in Egypt for many years: Herr Gerhard Bauch, agent of the German industrial company "Quandt." Lotz learned from the mouth of his intimate friend Kiesow — and discreetly checked the information with the chief of the mounted police — that Bauch used the "Quandt" company as a cover, a ruse known to Egyptian counter-espionage. Bauch was chief of the Middle East branch of the famous "Gehlen Organization," the strategic branch of Federal Germany's Intelligence Services, financed and supervised by the American C.I.A.

Named after a Nazi general, the ubiquitous "Gehlen Organization" spread its tentacles throughout East Germany and the Communist countries behind the Iron Curtain. Soon after Nasser's rise to power, General Gehlen concluded that the network he operated for the Americans—with the blessing of the Bonn Government—should be solidly implanted in the Middle East. The "Gehlen Organization" for the Middle East established its headquarters in Cairo. In the Middle East, as in Central and Eastern Europe, Gehlen's agents were primarily interested in developments inside the Communist camp, not in the Arab world. Their assignment was to glean information on Soviet Russia's growing ties with Egypt and Syria.

At year's end, in 1961, as Lotz launched his enterprise in Cairo, Gerhard Bauch, Gehlen Middle East agent, executed a masterly coup. Bauch arranged a deal with Colonel Mahmoud Halil, Chief of the Egyptian Air Force Intelligence.

Bauch would furnish Halil with information useful to the Egyptian Air Force. Halil would inform Bauch about the evolution of relations between Egypt and countries in the Soviet orbit. Halil learned much later, when it was too late to repair the damage, that data he supplied to Bauch not only landed on General Gehlen's table in Bad-Godesberg, near Bonn, but found its way to Israel's Intelligence Services in Tel Aviv.

Did Gerhard Bauch, loquacious compatriot of Tel Aviv's "Eye" in Cairo, collaborate in all innocence with his fellow countryman, the horse breeder in Israel's pay? Or was it at the suggestion, perhaps the orders of his superiors in Bonn that he tipped Lotz, with apparent negligence, on information of vital interest to Israel?

Egyptian authorities, years later, judged that the Bauch-Lotz collaboration could not have been fortuitious. "Bauch cooperated with Lotz with the full agreement of the West German Government," the Egyptian Court declared in 1965.

In July 1962, as Lotz's operations seemed to be functioning smoothly, he received a written message from Vienna summoning him to Munich immediately. Lotz made the trip with Waltraud. In Munich, Rudy gave Lotz an address in Paris, where he was to meet "Mr. Joseph."

On August 4, 1962, Lotz was crestfallen to learn that as a secret agent, he was a dismal failure. In a small furnished studio near Avenue de Wagram, "Mr. Joseph" received Lotz and dryly informed him: "I know that your business in Egypt is prosperous. I know that all Cairo comes to ride in your establishment, and that alcohol flows freely at your parties. I know you get information from the Gehlen people but you found out nothing about the essentials, and were incapable of informing us on what is important to us. Fortunately, we have agents more competent than you when it comes to really learning what goes on around Nasser."

Lotz, uncomprehending, remained silent as "Mr. Joseph" poured it on. "Two weeks ago, on July 21, to be exact, Nasser proceeded with the preliminary firing tests of two ground-to-ground missiles, assembled by your compatriots, the German scientists hired by Egypt. The very same ones who come to your fancy parties. And if you believe that Gerhard Bauch and company don't know about it, you are sadly mistaken."

Lotz was speechless. He realized that the information he had sent to Tel Aviv was of minor importance compared to this astounding news of the missile tests. Now he understood why Israel spent tens of thousands of dollars to maintain agents in Cairo; why it was crucial to Israel's survival to discover in time that missiles capable of destroying the Jewish State were being tested.*

Lotz spent three days in "Mr. Joseph's" company, giving him a detailed report of his activities in Cairo, telling about his adventures and talking at length about the influential people he knew. Since Lotz's report was tape recorded, "Mr. Joseph" meticulously sifted out information of value. He advised his agent which persons to cultivate, whom to avoid and to eliminate from his circles. But he insisted that Lotz, because he was German, should have no difficulty in introducing himself among German scientists in Cairo and gaining their confidence.

Having rebuked Lotz and set down the main lines of his activity in Egypt, "Mr. Joseph" explained that his agent's work in Cairo could be of the utmost importance to the country employing him.

"You have met with a serious failure. It is most regrettable, but those things do happen in our profession. You still enjoy my full confidence, and I am convinced that you will do better in the future," "Mr. Joseph" concluded.

"Mr. Joseph" gave specific orders. Lotz was to spend more money if necessary. He would thoroughly prospect the German colony in Cairo, and try to procure detailed results of the missile tests. He would return to Cairo with a new transmitting and receiving set, more powerful than

---

* It was only in June 1967, after the Six Day War, that Israel learned that the Egyptian missiles had not yet reached the operational stage. Western sources indicated that U.A.R. missiles were operative, but had been mysteriously sabotaged on the eve of the war.

the first radio which he must dispose of in the Nile River.

"Your girl, Waltraud, sees you transmitting messages. Did you tell her what we had agreed upon?" "Mr. Joseph" inquired.

"Waltraud thinks I'm supplying secret information to NATO," Lotz explained. Now that Waltraud was mentioned he pleaded with "Mr. Joseph" to allow him "at last" to marry her. "Mr. Joseph" agreed.

In September 1962, Wolfgang Lotz and Waltraud Noumann were married in Munich. They immediately returned to Cairo. In their trunk, Lotz packed a small bathroom scale for his bride's slimming diet. The scale hid a miniaturized transmitting and receiving radio.

A change had taken place in Lotz's work. "Mr. Joseph's" persuasive instructions in Paris had borne fruit. Early in October, he radioed the following message to Tel Aviv:

"Wish to meet Paris friend urgently."

Tel Aviv promptly answered:

"Friend expects you. Come immediately. Usual itinerary."

As usual Rudy met Lotz in Munich and told him where and when to meet "Mr. Joseph." An appointment was arranged for the next day in Paris, in an apartment in the sixteenth *arrondissement*. Lotz appeared at the appointed hour, and shaking hands with his chief, Wolfgang presented a complete, detailed list of the German scientists, engineers and technicians employed on the missile project in Egypt.

Lotz's list included more than forty names, providing

the Israelis with information they lacked: the private addresses of the German missile experts in Cairo and Helwan, precise descriptions of their specialties, and home addresses of their families in West Germany.

Lotz handed "Mr. Joseph" microfilm of top secret plans of the Egyptian armament plant near Helwan, whose code name was "3 3 3." When these plans were carefully examined by Israeli scientists, they assured their authorities they could breathe easier. Lotz's microfilm proved the failure of the Egyptian missile, designed and put into production by the German specialists from Pennemunde, where they developed the infamous V 1 and V 2 rockets. The Egyptian missiles, "El Zafer" and "El Zaher," were capable of transporting one-half ton explosive charges a distance of 200 to 400 miles. Theoretically they could "cover" all of Israel. At this stage of their development, as clearly indicated on the blueprints, these were "blind" missiles, lacking an electronic navigation system capable of guiding them to precise strategic targets of vital importance to Israel.

When Lotz returned to Cairo after a week of intensive consultations in Paris, he knew he had won the trust of Israeli Intelligence. Engraved in his memory was a new, complicated code. The new code would enable him to transmit, together with current news, figures, formulas, and details of technical and scientific data.

As 1962 faded into 1963, the splendid villa of Mr. and Mrs. Lotz, in an exclusive residential district, was fast becoming a temple of pleasure in the Egyptian capital. High society, Egyptian and German, happily accepted invitations to Lotz parties. Austerity, decreed by President Nasser, whittled away at the entertainment available to the smart set. Among the new guests seen at the Lotz parties was the Vice-President of the U.A.R., Nasser's right-hand man, M. Abdoul Latif El-Baghdadi. The Parliament's President, Anwar Sadat—who was to succeed Nasser in 1970—toasted Wolfgang in company with the Sabri brothers. Sabri had recently occupied a key role in the Egyptian Secret Services. Transferred to another post following discovery of a periodic "court intrigue" against the Nasserite regime, Ali Sabri was especially welcome at the Lotz home.

Lotz treated his guests magnificently. His parties always included elegant young women, ever willing to dispense their favors. Lotz skillfully steered cocktail talk to current news. Mrs. Lotz and the Kiesows helped gather the harvest of relevant information. Lotz's clandestine transmissions to Tel Aviv reported on the inner politics of Egypt, the condition of the economy, and military data. For the heads of the "Mossad"* in Tel Aviv, Lotz earned his nickname "Our Eye in Egypt."

One evening at a Lotz party, the spacious living room and the two adjoining rooms connected by the main entrance lobby, overflowed with guests. Many pressed around the heavily laden buffet.White-clad waiters moved through the crowd, presenting silver trays laden with refreshments and Oriental sweets. Western diplomats chat-

* "Mossad," the Hebrew designation of the center of Israel's Intelligence Services.

ted with Egyptian officials and officers. The Germans kept mainly to themselves speaking their Teutonic tongue.

Lotz unobtrusively on the alert, his eyes and ears open, noticed a young, pretty woman who was brought to the soiree by a cavalry officer. She was introduced earlier as a British tourist. Lotz did not catch her name. Lotz watched her. She was looking for something. Lotz lost sight of her for a moment. He picked his way through the chattering throng, searching for the girl near the buffet. Not seeing her there, he hurried towards the entrance hall, where latecomers and early-departing guests mingled. Between the entrance and the living room, a small room was used as a cloak-room. Instinctively, Lotz eyed the hanging rows of mink coats and officers' cloaks. At the far end of the double row, he caught the English tourist, rapidly searching the pockets of a man's light overcoat. Lotz quickly closed in before she noticed his presence, as she extracted an address book.

"You are nothing but a miserable amateur! Get out as fast as you can! Scram!" Lotz hissed, trying to forestall a scandal.

The young girl blushed, mumbled an excuse, returned to the living room, and a few minutes later, disappeared with her escort. Lotz presumed that she worked for Gerhard Bauch. Despite their association Lotz reported the incident to Tel Aviv. By now he transmitted from the maid's room, under the roof, not even bothering to hide the radio under the bathroom scale.

During his trial, Lotz was to learn that the "English" girl prowler had been called back to her country because of the cloakroom incident. She was spying for Israel, not Britain or Germany.

The archives of the Tel Aviv center of Israel Intelligence contain more than one hundred messages bearing Lotz's coded signature, all dated 1963. This is an indication of the amount of data that "Israel's Eye in Cairo" managed to transmit in one year, at the rate of two, or three transmissions a week. His information covered a wide field, from political evaluations to precise military details. It covered changes in the personnel and composition of Egyptian Government Services. This was carefully analyzed in Tel Aviv. While Lotz was considered a first rate "collector" of information, his superiors at the Tel Aviv center would not risk assigning him yet with an operational mission in the U.A.R.

A first attempt in this perilous field was made in April 1963.

This was a month after the arrest in Zurich by Swiss police of two men accused of being Israeli agents, the Israeli, Joseph Ben-Gal, 33, and the Austrian scientist, Otto Jockelick, 42. According to the charge sheet the Swiss Attorney General presented to the Basel Court during the trial in June 1963, Ben-Gal and Dr. Jockelick attempted to intimidate and threaten Miss Heidi Goercke, daughter of the famous German scientist, Professor Paul Goercke, then in the employ of Egypt's aeronautical industry. Ben-Gal and Dr. Jockelick were let off with a suspended sentence of two months. The verdict was annuled by the Appeals Court. The professor's daughter claimed she was intimidated to urge her father to return to Germany promptly, "to avoid any mishap befalling him." Ben-Gal and Dr. Jockelick were arrested that evening on their trip to Zurich from Basel.

Another episode which was unpublicized took place during the winter of 1962. Not until March 1963, did the German press reveal that attempts had been made to assassinate the German scientists working in Egypt.

On November 27, 1962, a registered letter stuffed with explosive material, mailed in Hamburg, was delivered to the home of Professor Wolfgang Pilz, director of the team of German scientists working in Cairo. Miss Hannelore Wende, the professor's secretary and intimate friend, opened the letter which exploded in her face, disfiguring and blinding her.

On November 28, a parcel labeled "scientific manuals" also mailed from Hamburg, reached the assembly plant of the "3 3 3" Egyptian missiles in Helwan. The parcel, handled by a member of the administrative staff, exploded, killing five Egyptian civilians.

On November 29, another parcel containing books, also mailed from Hamburg, arrived in Helwan. The Security Services, alerted and vigilant by the explosions of the past two days, X-rayed this "book parcel." They disconnected the detonator in time. A deadly load of explosives was found hidden in the hollow books. German police, with the agreement of the Egyptian authorities, suppressed news of all three incidents so as to aid the investigation begun in Hamburg. The arrest of Ben-Gal and Jockelick, implicated in an act threatening the safety of a German scientist from Cairo, broke the story in the press. Through official and unofficial channels, Israel demanded the withdrawal of German scientists from Cairo, launching a worldwide information campaign to expose their anti-Israel enterprise. President Nasser declared on April 2, 1963, in an interview granted to the Lebanese newspaper *El Mouharer*. "Israel sent those infernal machines to the German scientists working in Egypt, thereby killing six technicians. It is not the first time that Israel resorts to acts of criminal terrorism. Shortly before the Suez expedition of 1956, the Egyptian military attache in Jordan, Colonel Sala'h Moustafa, was killed in the same way. A parcel containing books was mailed to him through the good offices of Israeli secret agents, and exploded in his hands."

On the day Nasser accused Israel of mailing the explosives, Lotz and his wife flew to Munich. Lotz hurried to meet Rudy Bernstein, who had urgently called him through a radio message transmitted by the Tel Aviv center.

"Return to Cairo as fast as you can," Bernstein commanded, "in your luggage put a number of small soap cakes. They contain explosives. Have no fear. You aren't the one who will use them. Your task is merely to get them into Egypt."

Bernstein explained that Lotz would receive a message from Tel Aviv, naming a restaurant in Cairo. Lotz was to go there at the appointed hour and day, wearing a small blue and white scarf—which Rudy gave him. Two strangers would join him at his table. Lotz would lunch with them, chatting with these unknown people as if they were old acquaintances. At the end of the meal, the strangers would pick up the loaded soap cakes which Lotz, upon arriving, would deposit on an empty chair at his side.

When Lotz was arrested two years later by Egyptian counter-espionage, half a dozen Yardley soap cakes, filled with explosives, were found in his villa. The message Rudy told him to expect never came. Lotz, with characteristic German obedience to orders, did not rid himself of the soap cakes.

These soap cakes were among the exhibits submitted to the Cairo Court that tried Lotz in 1965. The Court President asked to look at them. The State Attorney objected that "Israel's infernal machines have already made too many victims in Egypt..." Lotz offered magnanimously to disconnect the fuses in front of his judges. The tribunal nervously rejected his kind offer, content to see the soap at a safe distance.

In March 1964, Lotz made another trip to Munich, where he met Rudy Bernstein and another Israeli agent. Lotz reported on the latest activities in meticulous detail. He received his instructions, and was asked to obtain the answers to precise questions about Egypt's armaments, and certain political figures. Rudy informed Lotz that it was premature to use the soap cakes. Lotz returned to Cairo, and succeeded in uncovering the answers to the questions asked by Rudy and his colleague.

In July 1964, Lotz left for Europe again, accompanied by Waltraud. From Munich, he took the plane for Paris, alone, to meet "Mr. Joseph." This time, contrary to the original intentions of the Tel Aviv center, Lotz was assigned to carry out an operational mission.

"The German scientists and technicians are developing jets for Nasser and are preparing to build supersonic fighter planes," said "Mr. Joseph." "Everything we have done to have them evicted from Egypt has not brought results. We rely on you, Lotz, to execute a daring scheme. It will surely have important repercussions on condition that it be perfectly executed."

"Mr. Joseph" promised Lotz a monthly salary increase of $ 200 and authorized him to buy a new Volkswagen.

"What should I do?" Lotz inquired.

"Scare the German scientists in Cairo," "Mr. Joseph" replied.

"How?"

"Return to Munich. A friend will phone you at your hotel. He will fix an appointment. You are to meet him. He will give you a certain number of envelopes, containing letters addressed to Germans in Cairo. Some of these letters will cause some damage to their addressees—damage of a very limited nature. Nothing really serious. All you need to do is to mail these letters when so advised. Take care to mail them from different post offices in Cairo, in order to blur the trail."

Lotz returned to Munich and received the expected phone call. Then a man Lotz had never seen before mumbled an incomprehensible surname and invited him to enter a black Mercedes and sit at his side. They drove without exchanging a word to a point about seven miles outside Munich. The stranger turned off the motor, got out of the car, and returned with an object carefully wrapped in rags and plastic which he extracted from the car trunk. He handed the package to Lotz, explaining: "Here's a cheese tray of a type currently produced in France. But this one is hollow. Inside, you will find six envelopes already addressed. You know what is expected of you. You are to mail these envelopes on September 20. For confirmation, you will receive a coded message that will begin with the word boots."

Lotz and Waltraud returned to Cairo on September 8, aboard an Italian ship. Their new Volkswagen was in the hold. Among the household goods imported by the Lotz couple, whom the customs officials at the port of Alexandria knew well, was a wooden cheese tray.

Ten days after their arrival, Lotz received the following message, "Boots. All is well. Date as decided on twentieth. Confirm boots."

On September 20, Lotz radioed confirmation in a message to Tel Aviv, "Boots sent today as decided. Boots."

Lotz had mailed the half dozen letters, not all containing light explosive charges, from post offices in different neighborhoods. These letters differently worded, admonished their respective addressees to leave the U.A.R. as fast as possible.

The letter addressed to technician Joseph Eisig stated: "We have the honor to inform you that your name is on the black list of the German scientists and technicians working for the Egyptian armaments industry. We know of your professional activity in the local aeronautics industry. Out of a sincere concern for the welfare of your wife, Ruth, your daughter Inge, and your son Peter, we urge you to leave immediately your work in Egypt and return to Germany. This is imperative. Think of the fate of your family."

Another letter, mailed to the aeronautical expert Ernst Stang, said: "We are informed of your activity benefiting Egyptian military industry. We are equally aware of all you are doing to strengthen the morale of the Egyptian population. You are mistaken in thinking you would not be able to find a job measuring up to your training and talents in some country other than Egypt. With a little good will, you could easily find work in Europe or Ghana. The fact that your contract expires in two years should not stop you. We urgently advise you to leave Egypt."

These letters, mailed by Lotz, carried the same mysterious signature, "The Gideonites." Gideon led the ancient Hebrews who vanquished the Midianites, twelve centuries before Christ.

A week after these letters were mailed, on September 27, 1964, the Center of Israeli Intelligence received the following message from Lotz: "The letter sent to the technician Kirmayer did not explode. Another letter exploded at the Ma'adi post office, wounding a clerk. All other non-loaded letters reached their destinations. The German colony is greatly upset. Additional information in later messages."

Three days later, Lotz transmitted to his superiors a complete list of technicians working for a large industrial concern in West Germany who had been engaged by the

Egyptian Government, and were preparing to move to Cairo. Forewarned, Israeli Secret Services acted quickly. They succeeded in preventing the departure of the new personnel. Lotz radioed the names and addresses of other German specialists working in Egypt. They eventually received threatening letters, some of which were loaded. All these letters were mailed in Cairo.

Contrary to the expectations of Lotz's bosses, not all the German scientists and technicians were intimidated by Israeli threats. Some left Egypt, but other technicians—Germans, Austrians, Swiss and Scandinavians—replaced them.

Only when political factors came into play was the German scientific colony in Egypt dispersed.

CHAPTER SEVEN

LUCK RUNNING OUT

Real-life spy thrillers spin to their denouement, turning like a wheel of chance, a throw of the dice, a haphazard accident, a stroke of fate, a random chance. It also happened in Syria, where Eli Cohen, Israel's "Man in Damascus," was caught at his transmitter sending the secrets of the innermost recesses of the highest circles of government. Eli Cohen's miniature radio waves were traced because they happened, by bad luck, to clash with the kilocycles used by the receiver of a foreign embassy which complained to the authorities.

In Cairo, Wolfgang Lotz ran out of luck because the United Arab Republic switched diplomatic allegiances from West Germany to East Germany.

Israel's "Eye in Cairo" was caught in the web of Soviet influence drawing Egypt closer and closer to Moscow and away from the West. When Soviet Premier Alexei Kosygin paid a state call on President Gamal Abdul Nasser in Cairo early in 1965, the Russian leader paved the way for the U.A.R. to officially invite the head of Communist East Germany, President Walter Ulbricht, to pay his first visit to Egypt.

Ulbricht's arrival in Cairo February 24, 1965, when he was welcomed by President Nasser with full ceremonial honors due a king, was a death blow to the hitherto smooth and friendly relationship between Egypt and West Germany.

Bonn's foreign policy since World War II was based on the principle that friendship with East Germany was inconsistent with diplomatic relations with West Germany. All nations had to choose between the two Germanys, but only Moscow was permitted to maintain official connections on both sides of the Berlin Wall.

Bonn reacted to Ulbricht's reception in Cairo angrily and coldly informed Cairo that its flirtation with Pankow meant automatic breaking of diplomatic relations, cancellation of West German financial and technical assistance programs, and termination of commercial and cultural arrangements.

Kosygin had pulled Nasser into the Communist trap. The results were debits for Egypt and credits for the Iron Curtain countries. Nasser, indebted to Moscow for military equipment in his endless confrontation with Israel, could gain little from the Soviet satellite in East Germany, compared with the material benefits of commercial ties with the booming West German "economic miracle." Losing Bonn as a diplomatic friend meant pushing the West Germans into the lap of hated Israel, which would celebrate lifting its informal relationships to full diplomatic recognition and exchange of embassies in Bonn and Jerusalem. Nasser, on the roller coaster of growing involvement with the Communist world, could not turn back. He submitted to the cutoff of relations with the West Germans.

One of Nasser's first decisions in the inevitable readjustment of his ties with the two Germanys was to secretly order the termination of the "Gehlen Organization's" activities in the U.A.R. Extending its tentacles under the adroit management of Gerhard Bauch, the "Gehlen Organization" served multiple masters. Radiating from its Cairo base, the "Gehlen" people spread through the Arab world, being received throughout the Middle East and Near East as though its Cairo home address was tantamount to official blessing from Nasser himself. The Egyptian Intelligence, in turn, utilized "Gehlen" agents to foment revolt and attempt pro-Nasserite coups in Syria, Iraq, the Yemen, Sudan, Libya, Jordan, Lebanon, Saudi Arabia and elsewhere in the Moslem world. "Gehlen" was a double eye for American C.I.A. operations countering Soviet expansion in the Middle East and for its parent government in Bonn.

"Gehlen's" many-faceted game was over. Egyptian secret police compiled lists of all German citizens residing in Egypt. The whole German colony was placed under surveillance. Every arrival of a visitor or tourist from West Germany was reported to the secret police. Every trip of a German out of Egypt was recorded.

The watch on the Germans began as part of the security precautions and preparations for Walter Ulbricht's State visit. Sensitive to East-West hatred and political antagonisms across the Berlin Wall, the Egyptian authorities became obsessed with the fear of assassination of the East German Communist chief.

Forty-eight hours before Ulbricht's scheduled arrival, Egyptian secret police threw a protective dragnet over the German colony in Cairo. Thirty Germans were quietly arrested in their own homes and taken to headquarters without a word of publicity in the newspapers or on the radio and television. Of the thirty arrested, all but seven were released after Ulbricht's departure.

The news blackout was strictly imposed upon the controlled Egyptian press and radio, and censorship blue penciled foreign correspondents and news agencies' reports of the arrests from the February 22nd roundup until March 4, 1965. The West German Embassy in Cairo was thrown into turmoil. Frantic appeals by families and friends of the imprisoned Germans flooded the switchboard at the Embassy. Formal and unofficial inquiries and protests by Embassy officials to the Egyptian Foreign Ministry evoked noncommittal replies and explanations about "preventive arrests" and indications that the detainees would probably be released after President Ulbricht's departure.

On March 4, the story broke in the semi-official newspaper, *Al Ahram*. A front page report foretold the changing winds blowing through German relationships in Cairo: "A number of individuals belonging to a German terrorist spy network were arrested at their respective residences by Egyptian counter-espionage services. It appears from what the suspects themselves admitted that the spy network in question was directed by Israel's Secret Services which utilized these German citizens. Israel had judged it was convenient to carry out acts of terrorism against German citizens residing in Egypt with the help of other Germans."

"There is no connection, however, between these arrests and the current crisis in the relationship between Egypt and West Germany. The fact that these arrests were carried out on the eve of President Ulbricht's visit is accidental. One of the suspects was caught preparing to flee from Egypt. The German consul has been authorized to visit the prisoners."

The next edition of *Al Ahram* and other Egyptian newspapers headlined the official announcement: "A German spy network serving Israel has been uncovered." The following names of spy suspects were published:

Wolfgang Lotz, 44 years old, former Nazi Wehrmacht officer, owner of a horse stable on the outskirts of Cairo.

Mrs. Lotz, nee Waltraud Martha Noumann, 35, German citizen who married Lotz in 1962.

Otto Noumann and his wife Klara, parents of Mrs. Lotz, residents of West Germany who were visiting their daughter and son-in-law in Cairo.

Frantz Kiesow, 47, representative of a German industrial company in Cairo, and his wife Nadia, 41, an Egyptian citizen who married Kiesow in 1951.

Gerhard Bauch, 39, representative of the German company "Quandt," in Egypt.

What happened? How did it happen? Wolfgang and

his wife and her parents, and the Kiesows and Gerhard Bauch, each in solitude and despair and shock, asked the questions and reviewed the past to search for answers.

Bauch, with Germanic thoroughness, replayed every step of the "Gehlen" operation under the Nasser regime in the wake of the ouster of the British in 1953. Bauch recalled the ideal state of collaboration with the Egyptians for almost a decade at every level of official contact, always under the approval of President Nasser whose aegis was channeled through Mahmoud Halil.

By 1962, Bauch felt the collaboration was cooling over the difficulties created by Israel Secret Service activities aimed at the German scientists, and utilizing Germans to threaten Germans in Egypt.

Egyptian authorities complained about Bonn's apparent lack of enthusiasm in assisting Cairo to trace the senders of explosives in the mail from Hamburg to Cairo and Helwan.

President Nasser and his General Staff and Foreign Ministry were angered by intelligence reports of clandestine arms shipments from West Germany to Tel Aviv. The Bonn Government obviously refrained from any overt anti-Israel act or policy which might be misinterpreted by Western public opinion, especially in the United States, as a retrogression to Nazism. The Egyptian Government had looked on helplessly since 1952 when West Germany inaugurated its reparations and restitution program to repay the Jewish victims of Hitlerism individually the equivalent of hundreds of millions of dollars and to buildup the Israeli economy with $ 800 million in reparations over a twelve year period.

The special relationship developing between Bonn and Jerusalem during the Adenauer and Ben Gurion administrations awakened suspicions in Cairo that the "Gehlen Organization" served not only Egyptian, German and American interests throughout the Middle East, but might possibly be funneling strategic information about Egypt to its enemy, Israel, which had inflicted the humiliating defeat of Nasser's armored forces in Sinai in one nightmarish week in October 1956.

Halil warned his friend one day over drinks, "Gerhard, beware! We know that Israel has a listening post somewhere between Cairo and Bonn."

Halil's warning reflected the growing nervousness among the rulers of Egypt. President Nasser had exacerbated the relationships with Bonn by raising an international scandal about West German supplies of tanks to modernize Israel's armored forces who had swept through the Egyptian Army in one hundred hours only nine years before.

When Nasser invited Ulbricht, Bonn retaliated by severing diplomatic relations with Cairo. The West German Government poured gasoline on the fire by dispatching a special envoy to Jerusalem to arrange for the exchange of ambassadors. This enraged the Egyptian President and he summoned his closest advisor and friend, Marshal Amer, and entrusted him with the top command of the Secret Service, with the special mission to smash the German "Gehlen Organization."

Marshal Amer succeeded beyond the dreams of the most rabid super-patriot in his service. Lotz was rounded up, along with thirty other Germans, as a routine gesture only because he was known to be a friend of the "Gehlen" people. None of Amer's intelligence officers, and certainly not Amer himself, expressed any suspicions of Lotz, whom they all knew as the genial and generous host at the lavish parties they enjoyed. Lotz was liked and admired by the intelligence people who shared a common interest in the equine breeds. As Marshal Amer confided to his aides, they really did not expect to find anything suspicious at Lotz' home which they knew so well.

Wolfgang Lotz, methodical and careful in the extreme, certain he had never erred to arouse any suspicions, was confident that he was above arrest, especially since he had so many intimate friends in high places.

Earlier in that fateful month of February 1965, Waltraud's mother and father closed their little shop near Stuttgart and traveled to Cairo for a visit with their daughter and son-in-law.

On the morning of February 22nd, Wolfgang, Waltraud, and the older couple crowded into the Lotz Volkswagen for a drive to the world-famous battlefields of El Alamein. The World War II officer in Rommel's Army re-lived the Battle of El Alamein as he guided his family over the sands where the British stopped the Nazi drive towards Cairo and Palestine twenty years earlier.

As the winter sun was setting in early evening, the tired family drove into Mohamed Haleb street, unaware

as they approached their splendid villa that it was surrounded by twenty policemen and plainclothesmen. The
police hid among the darkened bushes, trees and corners
until the Lotz and Noumann couples entered the house.
Wolfgang switched on the radio to listen to the news and
mixed drinks for four. Just as he was about to offer a
cocktail to his father-in-law, the front door was smashed
open and the living room suddenly filled with strangers,
some in uniform and some in mufti.

Why, what, who? Before he could even ask what it
was all about, Wolfgang Lotz was seized by three policemen, who forced his hands into handcuffs. The elder Noumann was overpowered by surprise and shock more than
by the strength of young and muscular officers of the law,
and meekly extended his hands to the metallic wrist locks.
Waltraud and her mother were in tears, the mother in
hysterics, as they submitted themselves to handcuffs, the
ultimate in indignity in this home where the elite of Cairo
society and the heads of ministries and army commanders
had kissed the hands of the gracious and lovely hostess
at so many carefree parties.

While the handcuffed quartet was held under heavy
guard in the living room, police and detectives fanned
into every room and corridor, ransacking shelves and
drawers, tossing clothes out of closets, searching for incriminating evidence.

Wolfgang Lotz thought hard and analytically. He had
no idea that this invasion of his house was part of a
countrywide net thrown around the "Gehlen Organization" and its known contacts. He did not know, of course,

about Bauch, Kiesow and many other German friends being arrested at that moment. Occupied only with his own espionage work, he concluded—wrongly—that he was the only object of counter-espionage action. He was sure in his own mind that this massive intervention by such a large number of law officers meant that his undercover role as an Israeli spy had been discovered, and this was the end of the road.

Certain that the price to be paid for his treachery to Egypt on behalf of the abominable Israeli enemy was death, Lotz calculated coldly, quickly, that he could only save himself by cooperating with his captors.

"I know you know everything," Lotz said to the officer in charge. "How can I now be of assistance to you gentlemen?"

"Show us your hiding places," gruffly ordered the commandant.

Lotz showed everything. He took the officers to where he kept the miniature short wave radio transmitter-receiver. He found the Yardley soap containing explosives. He handed over microfilm of Suez Canal locations which he had recently photographed. In a dozen hiding places in the furniture and behind pictures on the walls, he revealed eye-popping caches of money, totaling $ 75,000 in large denominations.

The Egyptian officers and detectives could not believe their eyes. They had expected, at most, to uncover a few incriminating documents or letters tying Lotz to the "Gehlen Organization."

Aghast at their lucky find, the Egyptians broke into

a babble of self-congratulations and predictions of pro-
motions, rewards and fame that would be their windfall.

Before them was the Israeli spy and paraphernalia,
the apparatus, the film, the sabotage material and the
money which he used to reveal Egypt's secrets to Israel
and fulfill Israel's missions in the ancient land of the
Pharaohs.

CHAPTER EIGHT

ON TRIAL

On March 7, 1965, Egyptian television viewers were startled by the announcer's excited introduction: "We now bring you a historic event! We present in person the mastermind of a network of German terrorists and spies who were arrested in our capital. This spy is called Wolfgang Lotz. He will confess what he has been doing in our country, against the interests and security of our people and our glorious nation. May Allah bless our courageous Security Services which once again emerged victorious in defeating the criminal plots of our enemies."

The camera zoomed in on Wolfgang Lotz. On the television screen, his face appeared pale and drawn. He hesitated, drew his breath and began to tell everything, in English:

"Since 1961, I have been spying for Israel in the United Arab Republic."

Lotz's face faded from the screen, and his wife appeared. She had been standing at his side. The camera caught her sobbing. Collecting herself, she sobbed, "I beg the Egyptian authorities to give us a last chance and allow us to start a new life."

The camera moved to the panel of newspaper and TV reporters who would question Lotz and his wife. He repeated what he had confessed to the inquisition of the Security Services. He was a German citizen, a veteran of the Nazi Army who fought in World War II on Egyptian soil at El Alamein against the British occupiers of Egypt. He was contacted by Israel Secret Service in West Berlin in 1960. He yielded to his desire to be placed in business as a breeder of thoroughbred horses in Cairo, and he paid the price by agreeing to serve as an Israeli spy.

Pressed for details, Lotz outlined his espionage activities: gathering and transmitting information about Egypt's military, political and economic development.

"I obtained classified information about launching pads for the Soviet ground-to-air missiles in the Suez Canal Zone and I sent this information to Tel Aviv," Lotz admitted in his accented English. "I gave Tel Aviv a detailed transport system description of the Cairo-Ismailia routes."

Asked by a reporter to tell about the threatening letters to the German scientists, Lotz replied, as millions of fascinated TV spectators watched, "These letters were entrusted to me in Europe. They were to be mailed in Cairo. This was to convince the German scientists that a secret organization was operating in Egypt to get them out of the country, by threat or by violence."

Lotz turned penitent, expressing remorse, regretting

his part in endangering and actually harming German compatriots and innocent bystanders. "To spy, to acquire information on one country for the benefit of another country, is one thing," he lamented. "To send letters containing explosives, with the intent of killing, wounding or blinding the recipients, is a terrible thing which I did not intend or want to do. What I did I did under duress. I was under orders; do it, or lose everything you built up in Cairo. When I learned that among the letters which I had mailed, some contained explosives, I resolved never to do it again, and if I was forced to, I would quit the organization."

A reporter asked him how he justified his service in the pay of Israel when Israel was using German reparations funds. How did he feel as a German? "It hurts me to think that part of the money which Germany pays to Israel as reparations was used to pay me, a German citizen, to spy on Egypt and to threaten German scientists here," Lotz bewailed bitterly. "Israel should use its own citizens for such work," he added. Suddenly he appealed to Germans: "German citizens, hear me. Never do what I did. Don't let yourself be trapped in the Israeli game. Don't be carried away by their promises of money and an easy life."

Another journalist inquired why Lotz spoke so openly and candidly on television.

"My activities have been known for a long time by Egyptian counter-espionage. When I was arrested and taken to headquarters, they showed me copies of all the secret messages I had transmitted to Tel Aviv. They showed me my file, detailing an exact record of all my comings and goings, meetings, telephone calls, trips, even the jokes I made. I might say here on my own, I am appearing here on television of my own free will. Nobody forced me to come here and say what I say. I have been under no pressure. The counter-espionage people have treated me well, indeed courteously. I invite the German journalists to visit me in prison and talk to me."

It was Waltraud's turn. She was asked what she knew about her husband's spy work. She knew he was gathering and sending secret information, but she thought all the time he was serving NATO, not Israel, she said.

She had nothing more to say about his work because she contended she knew nothing more about it. Her role was to entertain her husband's friends and assure that the parties were well-prepared and that everybody was happy.

Following quickly after the television interview, which caused a sensation throughout the country, and in the world press, the Government spokesman called a press conference to extract the maximum mileage out of the counter-espionage coup, with its international repercussions against Bonn and Jerusalem.

The Government spokesman underscored Lotz's testimony on TV that the State Security Services had been well aware of his espionage activities for years, and that little, if anything, escaped the vigilance of the guardians of Egypt. For the first time, the names of Elias Gordon, Rudy Bernstein and "Mr. Joseph" were injected into the story by the spokesman, who filled in the details of Lotz's recruitment, training, activities, arrest and confession.

The official version of the Lotz case, as described by the Government spokesman, omitted details of the exact information transmitted over the years to Tel Aviv. The spokesman instead emphasized and re-emphasized the "vigilance" of the Egyptian Security Services and gave the impression that Lotz had transmitted little of value to the Israel Intelligence Service.

The scenario of the television program and the press conference served as advance indication of what the Lotzes would face in the court trial.

The charge sheet was released to the press in April 1965, two months prior to the trial. Charged with spying for Israel, Lotz was indicted on three counts:

1. Endangering the security of the United Arab Republic by acts of espionage benefiting a foreign country which was in a state of war with the U.A.R.

2. Illegal possession of arms and explosives.

3. Attempted murder against German scientists and Egyptian citizens.

The U.A.R. Attorney General informed the press he would request the death penalty for Wolfgang Lotz, Israeli spy.

When the trial opened on June 28, only Wolfgang and Waltraud Lotz and their friend Frantz Kiesow stood in the defendants' dock. Waltraud's parents had established their innocence and had been permitted to return to Germany, distraught, frantic over the fate of their daughter and son-in-law. They were afraid to stay and although they wanted to be near their children in their hour of trial, they were inwardly relieved to be far and away from the oppressive atmosphere of Egypt.

Missing from the trial was the director-general of the "Gehlen Organization," Herr Gerhard Bauch. Arrested on the night of the "Gehlen" roundup, Bauch mysteriously disappeared from Egypt shortly before the trial, and his name was never mentioned again in the courtroom or press. Rumors swept the German colony that Bauch was permitted to sneak out of Egypt because he "knew too many skeletons in the cupboard;" . . . too many Egyptian officials in high places were implicated in past deals with the Germans.

Public interest in the Lotz trial was whipped to feverish excitement by the buildup with the television interview, the Government spokesman's press conference, and daily disclosures and speculation in the newspapers and on radio and TV. The Lotz trial was billed as "the most sensational espionage trial since the prosecution of the French diplomats in 1962."

The courthouse of the Supreme Court of State Security was an armed camp. Hundreds of rifle-bearing policemen and soldiers surrounded the courthouse and stood sentry on roofs of nearby structures.

The trial was prepared and staged as prestige-builder for the Security Service, the defender of the people and the Republic against internal enemies.

Press facilities were meticulously arranged to satisfy the requirements of the news gathering agencies, a swollen corps of foreign correspondents, and the local and overseas television and radio crews. This was to be a world-wide spectacle enhancing the inviolability of the Nasser regime and condemning the culpability of West Germany and the treachery of Israel.

To show the U.A.R.'s judicial fairness, the German colony was invited to be officially represented. In seats of honor sat Dr. Fiedler, West German consul; Dr. Bernard Steinbach, unofficial legal counsel and observer; and other prominent German residents.

Twenty minutes before the opening of the judicial proceedings, the three defendants were led into the courtroom, all wearing white, handcuffed and chained to their guards. The three defendants each wore dark glasses and appeared outwardly calm.

The three-judge tribunal was presided over by Justice Hassan Fahmi Bedoui who ordered each of the accused to approach the bench and take the oath to swear to tell the whole truth and nothing but the truth. *O, Justice, when expelled from other hiding places, make this thy dwelling.* Lotz remembered this from somewhere, he could not recall the source. He thought of it with bitter irony. Justice in Nasser's Egypt! But did he really deserve justice?

While these random thoughts raced through his head, the attorney for the defense, the Egyptian barrister Ali Mansour who earlier achieved notoriety defending French diplomats on spy charges, arose, addressed the Court, and requested a month-long postponement. Ali Mansour argued that he had received the security file on the case on June 22, only six days before, and he would need a month to study the 2,000 pages of evidence, information and exhibits, and prepare his defense. He noted that the file included the testimony already given by Mrs. Lotz' parents who had left the country; and Kiesow's wife who had been absolved of complicity and released before the trial. The State Attorney General, Samir Naggi, had no objection. The President of the Court, Justice Bedoui, announced postponement until July 27, 1965.

Not until the trial re-opened a month later did the accused trio learn what charges they faced. The month-long wait in prison had not changed them, at least outwardly as far as reporters and observers could note. Lotz's eyes were hidden behind thick sunglasses which he wore in the courtroom. His hands were free of handcuffs but his left leg was chained to his guard. He was neatly dressed in a white suit and tie. He listened unmoved as the charges were read by the Attorney General, who started by accusing Waltraud of "complicity in acts of espionage and terrorism." Kiesow was charged with one word, "espionage." There were no particulars. The Attorney General concluded with the charges against Lotz: "espionage and attempted murder." Lotz was accused of mailing the explosives which seriously injured Mohammed Raggab, a postmaster, and Martin Kirmayer, a German technician. The Attorney General demanded the death penalty for both Wolfgang Lotz and his wife. A sentence of fifteen years at hard labor was asked to be imposed upon Frantz Kiesow.

A battery of eight attorneys constituted the defense. Defense Counsel Ali Mansour was assisted by three

Egyptian and three German lawyers, with Dr. Steinbach as adviser and observer.

The Court President called Lotz to the witness stand and subjected him to a brief cross-examination. Invited by the Chief Judge to be seated, Lotz thanked him and declined, "I wish to be treated as any other person standing trial in Egypt."

The press and television corps were disappointed in Lotz's testimony, which revealed no new sensations, and traced old ground previously covered in the initial TV interview and in government press releases. He added the note that he disposed of his first transmitting equipment by throwing it into the Nile.

On a table near the judicial bench lay Lotz's radio equipment, the bathroom scale which concealed the radio, the microfilm of the Canal Zone, the explosive soap cakes, and six pencil plastic sticks of explosives which would have blown up the scale if tampered with.

When Lotz was asked by the Attorney General to relate the details of his trip to Munich to receive the special soap, the accused requested time to confer with his defense counsel. They whispered a few moments. Ali Mansour addressed the court and suggested that the soap testimony be heard behind closed doors. Presiding Judge Bedoui nodded approval, and adjourned the proceedings' to the following morning.

The secret testimony was leaked to the press which sensationalized the episode of "The Gideonites" mail threats and explosives sent to the German scientists and technicians.

When the trial was resumed in open court, Lotz returned to the stand with the television cameras focused upon him. The TV audience saw a different Wolfgang Lotz on the screen, shaken, perspiring, wiping his face repeatedly. The suave, composed, confident German horseman had lost his "cool." He was harassed, anxious, nervous and halting in speech.

One headline-making disclosure followed another.

Lotz was confronted with a file of copies of secret messages he had radioed to Tel Aviv, and instructions he received from "the home office," from 1962 to the day he was caught in 1965.

"I confirm," admitted Lotz, wearily, "that these are all the messages that I transmitted to Tel Aviv and were transmitted to me. I certify that these are exact copies of the messages. I was never subjected to pressure by the officers of Egyptian Security who have questioned me about this."

Lotz then asked that additional testimony be heard in camera. The newspapers later headlined, "SENSATIONAL REVELATIONS BY LOTZ OF ISRAEL-GERMAN-FRENCH SPY LINKS." The court was leaking news for maximum political effect to injure the image of Israel and its allies.

The prosecution turned to Lotz's imports and financial dealings. "I had good friends at the port of Alexandria, and these connections enabled me to bring in whatever I shipped from abroad, without any trouble from customs or inspection."

He verified that his financial dealings passed through the Deutsche Bank of Munich and its Cairo branch.

"My contract with the Israelis was to terminate in June this year," he told the court, "Unfortunately, I was arrested only a few months before my contract expired."

Colonel Gamal Aladin Alfrag, counter-espionage expert in radio communications, testified to the power of Lotz's tiny transmitter to convey its messages to Tel Aviv. "This is a technical marvel," declared the colonel. "It has the power to transmit on short wave beyond a range of 500 kilometers. This is within the range of Tel Aviv."

Colonel Alfrag testified that two coded messages, written in invisible ink, were discovered near the radio equipment in Lotz's home when he was arrested. The decoding key was also exhibited.

Frantz Kiesow and his wife, Lotz's neighbors, postal clerks, mounted police who frequently visited the riding school, took their turns on the witness stand, filling in details but not enlarging on the story which was already known to the public.

In secret session, an unnamed Intelligence officer was believed to have given expert evaluation of the military, strategic, economic and political information which Lotz had transmitted. Not a word of his testimony was leaked to the newspapers and TV.

In open session, the prosecution introduced Mohammed Raggab, the director of the post office in the swank suburb Maadi. The postmaster wore a bandage over his right eye. He testified that, being suspicious of mail addressed to the German scientists after they had received a number of bomb threats, he opened a letter addressed to one of them.

"I had the feeling that this envelope might contain explosives. I opened it carefully, exercising all the precautions we were instructed to take. But it exploded anyway in my hands. I am blinded for life in my right eye."

A tall, large-boned, strapping Arab, blind and one arm missing, was led to the witness stand by a policeman.

"I am Adul Salem Maneh," he introduced himself. "One day my brother and I were working in a stone quarry near the Pyramids. I saw what looked like a tree trunk and walked over to examine it. It had a wooden lid. I lifted it. An awful explosion. Here I am. I lost an arm. I am blind. Doctors say I am blind for life."

The Attorney General informed the Court, "It was a cache belonging to the German terrorists." He pointed to the defendants.

A specialist on explosives was called to the stand and told how a package, mailed in Hamburg, delivered in Helwan, exploded and killed five Egyptian employees at a scientific installation.

Waltraud Lotz was summoned to the witness stand. Wearing a light, plain summer dress, her eyes hidden behind dark glasses, she appeared drawn and haunted by dread of impending doom. Yet, the buxom blonde matron mobilized inner sources of strength and spoke up unflinchingly in the face of the intimidating array of judicial and police power embodied in this courtroom and obviously dedicated not to serve justice but to serve the political purposes of a show trial.

141

She protested her own innocence, but did not abandon her husband to his fate. "I am only a simple housewife," Waltraud began, "I only take care of our home. I have never done any of these things. I am not a spy. I did not mail letters which to my knowledge contained any harmful materials. I never tried to harm anybody. Wolfgang and I love each other. We desire only to live together in peace and quiet."

The prosecutor brusquely ordered the contrite woman to be specific about her part in the Cairo subversive operation. She recalled how she met Wolfgang, how they fell in love and left Germany for Egypt, settling down to the happy and affluent life organized around their equestrian enterprise.

"My part was simply to make our home a happy and pleasant meeting place for all our friends," she told the court. "My husband makes friends easily, and the many people who came to our riding school and took an interest in horse breeding came to our home and enjoyed our company and the company of mutual friends. Wolfgang is well liked by many people in this country who admire his knowledge of horses and his charm and humor."

From the judicial bench came an interruption. "What do you know and what did you know of your husband's undercover activities?"

"Until we were arrested, I never knew anything about it," she insisted, "My husband never told me anything, and I had no reason to be suspicious. He did tell me that aside from the riding club and the breeding, he had some sort of responsibility to an organization connected with NATO. But nothing more than that. And I myself never knew that he had any connection with Israel."

She lost her composure and sobbed out a plea of penitence. "Our lives are in your hands. I am innocent. My husband meant no harm to people in this country. Whatever happens to my husband, I love him. Let us be together again to live in peace and quiet and not to hurt anybody."

CHAPTER NINE

THE CITIZENSHIP BOMBSHELL

Two days after the trial resumed, Attorney General Samir Naggi interrupted the proceedings to ask the judges for permission to introduce new evidence.

"I have an important declaration to make before the Court with regard to additional information which has just reached me, and is of decisive import in connection with this trial," stated Naggi.

Granted permission to present fresh evidence, Naggi went on: "I have just received a letter from a person in West Germany who informs us that Wolfgang Lotz is not a citizen of West Germany, but is a citizen of Israel!"

The courtroom erupted with shouts, exclamations, oaths, the hammering of the jurists' gavel, and the bedlam of journalists racing to their telephones.

"According to this informer," Naggi continued, after the courtroom noise and turmoil subsided into quiet again, "Wolfgang Lotz is in possession of a German passport, a West German passport delivered in his name in the year 1960. But we are now informed that Lotz is a citizen of Israel. We are told that Wolfgang Lotz served in the Army of Israel, where he was a commissioned officer."

The Attorney General, savoring his sensation, slowly, deliberately added details, each word a treasure for world consumption. "My informant, whose name I cannot reveal in court, tells us that this information about Lotz being an Israeli citizen has been in the hands of the West German magazine *Stern* for some time. But *Stern* did not publish the story after the magazine publishers were visited in Hamburg by a high official of the Israel Ministry of Defense."

The courtroom heard a collective gasp of shock. Lotz, obviously flabbergasted, leaned over to Mansour and whispered in his ear.

Mansour arose and approached the judges. "My client is greatly upset by this letter that has just been introduced," Mansour said. "He denies that he is an Israeli citizen. In my client's name, I contend that the letter in question is a faked document, intended to induce the Court into error and place the defendant in an inextricable position. The letter is full of lies. Wolfgang Lotz was born in Mannheim, Germany, in 1921. He is a citizen of Germany. I request the Court to declare the letter as inadmissible evidence because it is anonymous, and therefore according to law is of no value unless the Attorney General reveals the identity of the mysterious informer."

The President of the Court asked the Attorney General if he could name the correspondent and call him as a witness. Samir Naggi replied, "Imperative reasons require that the informant remains anonymous." A jurist motioned to Lotz and asked him: "Wolfgang Lotz, where were you born?" "Your honor, I was born in Mannheim, Germany, in 1921," Lotz answered, his voice drained of strength.

"Did you ever live in Israel?"

"Never," Lotz said, his mouth dry, his throat tight.

Instead of sitting down, Lotz remained standing, as if hesitant about his next move.

"Your honor," he added after a moment of silence, "I admit that I did go to Israel, once, in 1964, and stayed there for six days. My superiors in Europe had ordered me to go to Tel Aviv and to receive instructions. I met with a man whom I only knew as Meir."

In September 1968, after the retirement of General Meir Amit as Chief of Israel Secret Services, his name was allowed to be published in the Israeli press for the first time.

After another brief silence, Lotz resumed speaking.

"I never possessed Israeli citizenship. I never served in the Israel Army. The only correct detail in the letter is the date of my birth."

The atmosphere in the packed courtroom was electric as Lotz paused and talked again.

"I can guess at the reasons which impelled the anonymous letter writer to spread this calumny about me. I am prepared to tell the judges in closed session what these reasons are."

The judges conferred together and agreed to go into secret session again. The Court adjourned. The public and the press were requested to leave. For half an hour, the jurists, the attorneys and Court attaches held a closed session to hear Lotz's secret testimony.

Lotz and his wife left the courtroom by a side exist, escorted by their regular armed platoon. Lotz was pale and tired, leaning on Waltraud's arm for support as they walked to the armored car.

The sensation of Lotz's alleged Israeli citizenship died as suddenly as it was born. Not a word of it was mentioned in Court the next day or for the remainder of the trial.

No mention was made in the local press of what might have transpired at the secret session. Not until the Lotz couple were freed three years later did the West German magazine *Stern* reveal the inside story of this suppressed evidence.

Stern reported in 1968 that Lotz, in secret session July 29, 1965, had admitted his Israeli citizenship and testified against himself that he used his German citizenship as a native of Germany to cover up his espionage work in Egypt. *Stern* claimed that Lotz told the secret session of the Court that Egyptian counter-espionage knew that Lotz was an Israeli citizen from the time they arrested him.

"Egyptian counter-espionage chose to play the game, and played it to the end in considering the Israeli spy as a German citizen," Stern commented, "The Egyptians probably had reasons for doing this which were beyond Lotz's understanding. It was the Egyptian Government, at the highest level, and not the Egyptian counter-espionage organization which made the decision to hide the truth about Lotz's Israeli citizenship."

Not until Lotz's release in 1968 did *Stern* reveal the full story of its investigation into the life and background of Wolfgang Lotz. The German magazine assigned its ace reporter, Wolfgang Lohde, to the case when the news broke of Lotz's arrest in Cairo.

Lohde immediately inquired at the Bonn Interior Ministry about Lotz's identity. Lohde was referred to the civil registry at the Mannheim Municipality where Lotz was born. There, Lohde learned from the records that Lotz was born in Mannheim in 1921, and emigrated to Palestine with his mother in 1933, soon after his father's death. The file revealed that Wolfgang Lotz and his mother had registered claims in Haifa for restitution from the West German Government for losses of family property confiscated by the Hitler Government, and for Wolfgang's interruption of schooling at the age of 12. The restitution application showed that Wolfgang Lotz continued his education in Israel, then called Palestine. Wolfgang joined the pre-State Haganah defense organization as a youth, fought in the newly-established Israel Army in the 1948 Israel-Arab War of Independence, was promoted to lieutenant, and after the war worked on the administrative staff of the Haifa oil refineries.

When the State of Israel was established in 1948, Israeli citizenship was conferred upon Wolfgang Lotz as it was on all its residents, whether born in what was Palestine before 1948, or after immigrating to the Holy Land. For Israel is a land of immigration, with 1,400,000 of its inhabitants having been ingathered from the four corners of the earth.

Lohde also learned from the Lotz file that Wolfgang later moved to Jaffa from Haifa, and left Israel June 19, 1960, to settle in West Berlin. Wolfgang's mother, an actress who at one time was a member of the Israel National Theater, Habimah, and later was a teacher of English, also had emigrated from Israel and settled in Munich, living on the restitution payments she received monthly from the West German treasury.

Lohde went to Munich to interview Frau Lotz. Pleasing her with a gift of an elaborate historical album of dramatic art, she in exchange offered the *Stern* reporter a color portrait of her son, and spoke freely about his boyhood in Mannheim, his new life in Palestine, his military service in Haganah and in the Israel Army, and his postwar work at the Haifa refineries.

Frau Lotz may have informed the Israeli consul in Munich that she had been interviewed by *Stern* magazine, for the Israeli authorities intervened with the magazine publishers before they could get Lohde's story in type. They convinced the publishers that publication of Lotz's Israeli background would prejudice his defense in Cairo, and also implicate Israel and West Germany as collaborators in anti-Egyptian espionage.

Egypt's sudden cover-up of the Israeli citizenship revelation in court was believed to have emanated from the top level of the Foreign Ministry and the Presidential office which saw that exploitation of Lotz's Israeli background would be inimical to the U.A.R. claim for leadership of the Arab world. Only a half year earlier, Cairo propaganda was belittling the Syrian leadership for permitting Eli Cohen, Israel's "Man in Damascus" to penetrate the highest circles of government and expose the innermost secrets of the Syrian Army and the regime to the ears of Israeli Intelligence. President Nasser could not bear the thought of Syria striking back with ridicule at Egypt's negligence in allowing an Israeli spy to operate freely for more than three years in the shadow of his palace. The tribunal's suppression of the "anonymous" letter, on political grounds, protected the identity of its author. Lohde's indefatigable investigation connected the Lotz case with a Munich attorney by the name of Herr Seidel, who had been engaged to protect the interests of German scientific people working for Egypt. Seidel had handled the legal proceedings involving the bomb threats and attacks on the Germans. Among the accusations against Lotz was one that he had dropped the letters in the mail boxes.

Lohde also learned that Lotz was not recruited by Israeli Intelligence in West Berlin. He had traveled from Israel to Berlin in 1960 to establish residence and obtain a West German passport and identity card as a native of Germany. Under consular agreements between West Germany and Israel, citizens of Israel who were born in Germany were permitted to acquire dual citizenship in both countries. The *Stern* magazine investigator also found out that Lotz, a horse-lover since childhood, had been a riding master in Israel, and not in West Berlin.

Digging into Wolfgang's life history, Lohde learned

that Wolfgang's father was of Jewish parentage but had never identified himself as a Jew or associated himself with the Jewish community in Mannheim. When Wolfgang was born, he was not circumcised according to the Jewish tradition. The boy was reared until the time he left Germany for Israel at the age of twelve as a non-Jew.

Only an uncircumcised Israeli could be entrusted with the perilous espionage assignment of posing as a German in the land of the Pharaohs. The fiction of Lotz's German citizenship was protected even by the Egyptian Government which clamped the lid of official and press secrecy on the Seidel letter once it was introduced in court. The defense relied on the fiction of Wolfgang Lotz as an officer in Hitler's Army under Rommel's command at El Alamein to plead for leniency from the Egyptian Judges.

The final witness was Frantz Kiesow. Refusing to testify against himself, the grey-haired, pink-faced German stated flatly, "I am not a spy. I was never a spy. I never cooperated in any espionage. I reject the accusations against me. I did not transmit secret information concerning the Egyptian Army to my firm 'Mannesmann'."

Kiesow, the Cairo representative of "Mannesmann," stood unmoved during cross-examination and did not implicate himself with his own words.

On August 4, after a week of testimony, the Attorney General summed up his case for the State.

Elegant, commanding attention by his audacious speech, like a leading man center stage, Samir Naggi addressed the tribunal:

"Wolfgang Lotz was not alone as an Israeli spy in

our midst. I shall now reveal that a woman was spying for Israel among us. Her name is Mrs. Cornelia Walter. Her husband is a professor of archeology at Yale University in the United States. Last year, this woman came to our country under the guise of an archeologist, as a member of a party of other archeologists and historians who came here to visit our historical sites. Mrs. Walter became friendly with one of our army lieutenants. Through him, she managed to slip into circles of army people and officials in our military industries. She was far more interested in our missile development than in our Sphinx at Giza. She sought to contact the German scientists working on weapons development. Her activities and questions were duly reported to our Security Services by the lieutenant who accompanied her."

"The lieutenant took this woman to one of Lotz's parties. Apparently, she didn't know Lotz was working for Israel, and Lotz didn't know she was an Israeli spy. Something happened when they met face to face in Lotz's home that aroused Lotz's suspicions. She left the house in a hurry with the lieutenant. The next day, Lotz transmitted a radio message to Tel Aviv reporting the presence of this woman in Cairo. The message read, 'She behaved in my house like a bungling novice.' This is a copy of the message."

"Mrs. Walter was immediately ordered out of Egypt. Two days after she was at Lotz's house, Mrs. Walter left Cairo for New York. This shows us that Wolfgang Lotz had great influence on Israeli Intelligence Services, and that Israeli Intelligence placed trust in him. This man, this defendant Lotz is no ordinary spy, who was recruited for an ordinary assignment in Cairo. He is a dangerous espionage agent and saboteur, cunning and shrewd, a grave threat to our security."

The Egyptian press, radio and television seized upon this belated disclosure to interpret the Cornelia Walter episode as an anti-American turn by the Nasser Government. This interpretation was enhanced by the startling arrest, two weeks before the Lotz trial, of the editor-in-chief of the Cairo daily newspaper *El Ahbar,* on charges of spying for the United States and plotting to assassinate President Nasser.

Anti-Americanism was rife, pervading the political atmosphere in Cairo to the point where Washington felt it necessary to issue a formal denial that Mrs. Walter was serving as an American spy, or that she was even a United States citizen, or that her husband was a U.S. citizen, even though he was a member of the Yale faculty.

The Attorney General's savage summation of the case against Wolfgang and Waltraud Lotz thundered on for two full court sessions.

Reaching a crescendo of invective against the defendants, the state prosecutor demanded the death sentence for Lotz, and for his wife.

The case against Wolfgang Lotz, he declared, was unassailable.

As for Mrs. Lotz, the prosecutor added, "She actively aided and abetted her husband in espionage against our nation. Without her help, he could never have fulfilled his nefarious mission against the security of our country.

Waltraud Lotz, ever since 1962, has been serving as an operative for the Israel Secret Service, and shared full responsibility for the crimes of her husband."

The chief defense attorney, Ali Mansour delivered his summation on August 10, not as a plea of not guilty, but an appeal for clemency.

First, he took up the case of Waltraud Lotz. "It was her love for her husband that led Mrs. Lotz to come to our country, to work alongside him in the horse business, to entertain, but always without knowledge that he was working for Israel against us. She committed no crime other than loving him and making a home for him. I appeal to the court for the acquittal of Waltraud Lotz on the grounds that she was innocent of the charges read against her."

Years later, Lotz and his wife would laugh about something Ali Mansour had said at the trial: "Wolfgang Lotz could not possibly tell his wife he was working for Israel, knowing that Waltraud was profoundly anti-Semitic, and loathed the State of Israel."

Mansour's defense of Wolfgang Lotz attempted a justification, and sought an amelioration of his certain punishment, rather than trying to sum up a case of innocence.

"Your honors," the Chief Defense Attorney addressed the tribunal, "you see before you a former German soldier who fought on our soil in the Great War against the British who were occupying our country and who were driven out by our great leader. When the Great War ended, Wolfgang Lotz, with millions of other German soldiers, was part of a defeated, broken army, and their German nation was in disgrace and cut in half. Lotz, like other German soldiers returning home, had no home, no work, no future, no national pride. He left Germany and went to Australia in search of work and a new life. There he worked as a truck driver, but he led an unhappy existence in Australia and returned to his native Germany. He finally found work as a riding master, and in this occupation which he liked, he met the Zionist agents who took advantage of his love for horses and offered him a riding stable and a horse breeding business in Cairo if he would perform espionage services for them.

"The Zionists cleverly exploited the German defeat and guilt complex for the Nazi murder of many Jews. This is one of the ways the Zionists enlisted Lotz, along with the promises of putting him in a lucrative business in Cairo, with unlimited expense accounts.

"Lotz could not say no to the lure of living an affluent life while engaging in his favorite hobby, and he felt that by working for Israel, he as a former German Army officer, could expiate his guilt about the Nazi murder of the Jews.

"By cooperating with our Security Services in their investigation, Lotz has shown contrition for harm he has done our nation and the Arab cause. The principal culprit in this trial is not Wolfgang Lotz but the State of Israel. The Zionist State serves as the springboard for all the aggressions against our country and the Arab world. From Tel Aviv come spies and terrorists to infiltrate the Arab nation. Tel Aviv will continue spying and launching terror and aggression until that day when a united Arab nation will rise to annihilate the Zionist abomination in our Arab body and return Palestine to our Arab brothers. May Allah soon bring that victorious day to pass!

"Wolfgang Lotz stands guilty before you, but in view of the circumstances of his life, I present a plea for mitigation of the harshness of his sentence." Ali Mansour concluded.

Between the end of the Lotz trial on August 10, and the reconvening of the tribunal to deliver the verdict on August 21, Egyptian-West German relations underwent another radical change.

The Egyptian Government indicated to the Bonn Government through the good offices of intermediaries that Cairo desired a resumption of diplomatic relations which had been severed by West Germany when the East German Communist Chief Ulbricht visited Egypt. At the same time, those Arab states which followed Nasser's lead also expressed willingness to restore normal relations with Bonn.

West German newspapers took the hint and suggested in their comments on the Lotz trial that it seemed unlikely that Egypt would exact the death penalty against German citizens. The German press highlighted the understanding expressed by Defense Attorney Mansour for the German postwar psychology and his plea for leniency toward the Lotz couple. Egyptian newspapers quoted these comments in the German press to prepare the U.A.R. public and the Arab world for a surprise.

156

The Citizenship Bombshell

The August 21st court session required only ten minutes to decide the fate of Wolfgang and Waltraud Lotz and Frantz Kiesow. The courtroom was packed with journalists and television technicians and radio people.

A dozen German scientists appeared at the court for the first time. None had attended the previous trial sessions. Mrs. Nadia Kiesow carried a huge bouquet of flowers which partially concealed her elegant gown. She had learned in advance that it would be a day of celebration of Frantz's acquittal.

Wolfgang and Waltraud sat together, nervously holding hands for mutual comfort and encouragement. Kiesow, calm and assured, kept aloof from the Lotz couple, and did not say a word to them.

At nine a.m., the President of the Court read the verdict. The preamble stated that Wolfgang and Waltraud Lotz had been committing continuous criminal acts of espionage against the United Arab Republic since 1962, from their home in the Cairo area, on behalf of Israel Secret Service. The indictment of implication with the bomb threats and mailing of explosives to German scientists, and the casualties inflicted upon innocent Egyptians was reviewed and reaffirmed as proved in court.

The Court President read out that Lotz's repentance and cooperation with Egyptian Security Services were taken into account.

"These facts cannot excuse the accused," the verdict continued. "The Court did take them into account. Consequently, Wolfgang Lotz is hereby condemned to imprisonment for the rest of his life to serve his sentence at hard labor. The condemned is also required to pay a fine of EL 32,539, as compensation to Egyptian citizens wounded and incapacitated by acts of terrorism committed by the accused. Furthermore, all the property owned by Wolfgang and Waltraud Lotz is to be confiscated by the State."

Waltraud, adjudged guilty of aiding and abetting her husband's crimes of espionage, was sentenced to three years imprisonment at hard labor, and fined EL 1000.

Frantz Kiesow was freed. "It is true that Frantz Kiesow supplied data concerning the economy of the U.A.R., but we believe he provided this information in good faith, without intention of harming the nation," the Court declared in explanation of the acquittal.

Nadia Kiesow burst into tears of happiness. Frantz Kiesow smiled with relief and liberation. Wolfgang Lotz sighed as the oppressive burden of fear of execution was lifted from his heart. He was sad about his wife's three-year prison sentence; yet, glad it was not worse. Waltraud held back her tears.

The German scientists ducked out of the courtroom, evading reporters and TV interviewers who tried to record their reactions to the verdict.

News of the surprise verdict was a sensation in Egypt, in Germany, in the Arab world, and created an image everywhere of Egyptian humanitarianism and moderation. The Court fulfilled its political objective of establishing a friendly atmosphere in West Germany for resumption of diplomatic relations.

After the correspondents and the local press had ex-

158

tracted the last drop of ink from the Lotz story, it subsided and disappeared into oblivion with the removal of Wolfgang and Waltraud Lotz to the obscurity and deadly monotony of incarceration in the Cairo Central Prison. Frantz and Nadia Kiesow departed from Egypt, as he terminated his twenty years as representative of "Mannesmann" Steel Corporation of Germany.

A brief news item one day reported that Wolfgang Lotz, convicted spy, had suffered a heart attack and was transferred to the prison hospital. A piquant sidelight to this intimate story of the Lotz couple is that Mrs. Lotz was allowed to visit her husband once a week in the office of the prison warden, and in fact became pregnant and underwent an abortion in prison.

The Six Day War of 1967 changed the history of the Middle East and led to the eventual release of Wolfgang and Waltraud Lotz.

More than five thousand Egyptian officers and soldiers, including nine generals, were captured by the Israel Army as it swept through Sinai in three days to the Suez Canal.

The Egyptian war prisoners were held in Israel while Jerusalem and Cairo negotiated through the International Red Cross for an exchange. Israel demanded in return for over 5000 Egyptians the release of a handful of Israeli pilots and navy frogmen captured by the U.A.R. during the lightning war. And in addition, Israel insisted upon the release of a small but publicly undisclosed number of Israeli espionage agents, the list being headed by Mr. and Mrs. Lotz.

When President Nasser and his Security Service chiefs balked at freeing Wolfgang Lotz, the Jerusalem Government suggested to Dr. Gunnar Jarring, the United Nations mediator who was making the rounds of Middle East capitals in search of a peaceful solution, that he intervene during his visit to Cairo and attempt to negotiate Lotz's release.

Jerusalem held back on the nine Egyptian generals as the price for Lotz's freedom.

The generals, all representing leading families in Egypt, exerted their own pressure for their release.

The Cairo newspaper voice of President Nasser, *Al Ahram,* explained why the espionage agents were released: "We accepted release of the Israeli spies under pressure of our prisoners' families who wanted them home again. In any case, a spy who has been arrested and sentenced, is a 'dead' spy insofar as his ability to injure us again. He is of no use to us. Neither can he be of any use again for Israel after his anonymity has been destroyed forever."

Eight months after the Six Day War, as part of the prisoner exchange at Kantara on the Suez Canal, Wolfgang Lotz and his wife were released from Cairo Central Prison, driven to Cairo West International Airport, placed aboard a Lufthansa airliner for West Germany and the Egyptian chapter of their lives was closed.

Their mysterious disappearance during the Athens stopover was an Israeli Secret Service sleight-of-hand to save them from another trial in West Germany for bombing attempts on German citizens working in Egypt.

CHAPTER TEN

A SPY IN THE SINAI

Wolfgang Lotz was behind bars in Cairo's Central Prison from 1965 to 1968, but President Nasser kept warning his people that, as he put it, "Israel Secret Services continue to operate in the United Arab Republic."

Now it can be told that Nasser was right, at least to the extent of the remarkable story of an Israeli secret agent who occupied a sensitive post in Egyptian Army communications during the 1967 war in Sinai.

When the Six Day War ended, we had an opportunity to visit the Sinai battleground between June 11-18. The burning tanks were still smoking and the bodies rotting until mass burials laid 20,000 Egyptian officers and soldiers to rest under the hot sands of Sinai.

One burial of an Egyptian was different from all others. It was attended by a small group of high-ranking Israel Army officers who had reason to pay their respects to a U.A.R. soldier.

He was known to us only by his first name, Suleman. He was a captain, a specialist in radio communications. Years before the Six Day War, Suleman had been recruited in Cairo by the Israeli Secret Service agents to transmit vital information to Tel Aviv whenever war broke out between Egypt and Israel.

Suleman, a brilliant young man who was graduated from technical high school in Cairo and studied advanced courses in communications, had been overheard expressing dissatisfaction with corruption and disloyalty in the Nasser regime. Approached by an Israeli agent and invited to "talk over a bottle of Arak," Suleman poured out his opposition to Nasser's policies of mobilizing Egypt's meager resources for endless war against Israel, starving the masses of his people, and failing to fulfill his pledges of socialist reconstruction which would uplift the living standards, education, health and culture of the Egyptian nation.

Suleman had gained access to Western publications which reported Israel's achievements in raising the living standards of its people to European levels, bringing up a new generation of educated, skilled, dedicated young people who had proved in the 1956 Sinai War that they had the spirit, the morale and the technical and military superiority to defeat Egypt with fifteen times the population of the Jewish State. Suleman admired these achievements and believed that if Israel and Egypt could live side by side in peace, his own people would greatly benefit from such amity and cooperation for mutual benefit.

This was the thinking of a young Egyptian radio expert that brought him into the Israeli fold to serve the Jewish State, against the military interest of his own country, in the event of war.

A Spy in the Sinai

Suleman underwent secret training and indoctrination in Cairo, and was encouraged to advance as far as possible in radio communications and in ingratiating himself into high ranks in the U.A.R. armed forces.

His instructions were as follows:

Suleman would radio information to Israel only if and when he was transferred to the Sinai Peninsula.

He would utilize only regular army radio equipment.

His information to Israel would be as all-inclusive of wide-ranging Egyptian movements as he could possibly obtain.

Suleman, who had risen to the rank of captain by the time the 1967 war erupted, transmitted his first message to Israel Army intelligence on May 17, 1967, when Nasser mobilized his armed forces to take their battle positions in the Sinai Peninsula. Suleman listened in on radio instructions between various Egyptian units and commands, and headquarters in Cairo. He gained an overall picture of the Sinai movements and broadcast them in code to Tel Aviv. His transmissions were interrupted by activity in his own communications center, but he kept at the double job in between sending and receiving messages for his command.

From May 17 until the Israel Air Force devastated Egyptian airpower on the fateful morning of June 5th, Captain Suleman broadcast invaluable, detailed information about Egyptian troop movements, concentrations of strength, battle plans, commanders' instructions, and overall strategy to Israel headquarters in Tel Aviv.

All this time, he fulfilled his own assignments faithfully for the U.A.R. command in his sector, maintaining a steady flow of internal communications while interspersing them with external code messages to Tel Aviv.

On June 5th, Captain Suleman heard the roar of Israeli warplanes speeding toward their targets at U.A.R. air bases.

Out of the chaotic, disorganized babble from the devastation that had visited the Egyptian Air Force in the first three hours of June 5, Captain Suleman collated as concise a summary as was possible of U.A.R. aircraft losses and disabled airfields and transmitted the news to Tel Aviv.

On June 5, Israel armored forces struck across the Gaza-Sinai border line and smashed the Egyptian defenses, rolling down the axis roads towards the Suez Canal.

On June 6, Egyptian resistance was broken and Nasser's Sinai Army was in chaotic disarray, some units fighting back in retreat, other units abandoning their tanks, vehicles and weapons, and running barefoot over the sands.

On June 7, Israeli tanks broke through the Mitla Pass barrier and raced to the Canal, while other columns reached the international waterway along the northern route at Kantara.

Captain Suleman radioed the tangled threads of Egyptian defeat and disorder to Tel Aviv, clarifying the picture for the Israeli High Command which sought a clearer understanding of the magnitude of the rout and the ability of enemy forces to regather, if possible, for counter-attacks and last-man holdouts. Only in rare places did the Egyptians make last stands.

Suleman's last message was radioed on the final day of the Sinai battle. As Egyptian dreams of conquest were shattered by the Israeli blitzkrieg, Suleman's communications unit found itself trapped in a traffic jam of wrecked tanks, trucks, half-tracks, jeeps and supply vehicles in the narrow Mitla Pass between high, jagged stony cliffs.

Wave after wave of Israeli warplanes had relentlessly bombed, strafed and rocketed the retreating columns of Nasser's vaunted armored forces. As they piled up in a monumental traffic jam at the Mitla Pass, they were sitting ducks for the Israeli pilots who poured it on, setting entire mechanized columns afire.

Behind the Mitla Pass, Israeli tanks had penetrated to cut off the Egyptians' retreat to the Canal.

Captain Suleman received a code message from Israeli field radio communications.

"Where are you? Give us your exact location. We will keep our planes away from you."

"I'm in my unit's radio communications car, on the southern end of Mitla Pass, close by the Parker Memorial. I am expecting you," Suleman radioed back.

It was too late. Before the Israeli Air Force attackers could be called off the Mitla Pass, new waves blasted the pileup of vehicles again, and one of the targets hit was Captain Suleman's radio post.

When the shooting was stopped in Sinai by a UN cease-fire that night of June 7, an Israeli parachute unit was dropped at Mitla to search for Captain Suleman. His shattered body and smashed equipment were discovered. Identification was verified by his papers.

Headquarters was notified. A saddened group of Israeli officers gathered at the Mitla Pass, near the Parker Memorial, to bid farewell to an Egyptian who had played a vital role in Israel's victory.

PART III

EGYPTIAN SPIES

CHAPTER ELEVEN

LUK — MAN IN A TRUNK

A United Arab Airlines Comet jet glistened in the rain on runway number six at Rome Fiumicina Airport. It was 4.50 p.m. November 18, 1964, and Italian porters were completing the loading of passenger baggage into the hold. Takeoff had been postponed, two hours to 5 a.m. on the Cairo-bound non-stop flight.

A delivery truck, bearing the insignia of the United Arab Airlines, roared up to the plane, turned under the wing and screeched to a stop, skidding on wet asphalt. Two airline officials jumped out of the truck cab, hailed the porters, and ordered them to unload a trunk from the van into the plane.

The porters interrupted their handling of the luggage, and approached the truck. They looked at the trunk and it was larger than anything they had seen in their work. It was five feet long and two feet wide. On all sides were pasted big labels in English, French and Arabic: "Diplomatic Pouch. U.A.R. Embassy, Rome. Destination, Ministry of Foreign Affairs, Cairo."

"Diplomatic Pouch" — diplomatic immunity extends

to persons, packages, and mail, so the trunk was delivered directly from the Egyptian Embassy in Rome to the airliner.

"Hurry up," one of the U.A.R. officials commanded the porters, "Load this trunk as fast as you can. This plane is ready to leave."

The porters were puzzled by the order to place the trunk in the animals' hold, instead of the luggage compartment.

Sweating to get a firm hold on the trunk, which seemed to weigh hundreds of pounds, one of the porters thought he heard a strange noise, something like a muffled groan inside the outsized "Diplomatic Pouch."

He held the trunk handle tightly and put his ear closer. The moans, barely discernible, persisted. What kind of a weird animal were the Egyptians shipping in a "Diplomatic Pouch," the porter wondered. While the other porters were getting into position to lift the trunk out of the van and wabbling with their heavy load toward the plane, the suspicious porter slipped away and accosted an Italian Customs Inspector who was busy watching the loading of the last pieces of suitcases and travel bags into the luggage compartment.

"I heard something moaning inside the trunk, like a cat meowing," the porter whispered to the Inspector.

The Inspector approached the U.A.R. officials. "Would you mind," the Inspector asked them, "what's in the trunk?"

"Musical instruments," the senior Egyptian official replied.

170

Luk—Man in a Trunk

The Inspector put his ear to the trunk. He too heard faint moans, that sounded like screams for help.

"Stop loading," the Inspector countermanded the porters. He dispatched the suspicious porter to summon the Chief Inspector.

As he faced the alert porter, the Inspector was blocked by the senior U.A.R. official, while the other Egyptian pushed the trunk back into the rear of the truck. Both officials jumped onto the truck, and before the porters and the Inspector could react the vehicle sped away. The Inspector ran toward a red Alfa-Romeo parked off the runway, calling for another customs official nearby to follow him. Their Alfa-Romeo quickly overtook the U.A.R. truck on the airport highway leading to Rome, and the Inspector forced the truck over to the side. The Italian officials placed the diplomats under arrest, over their loud, excited protests proclaiming their diplomatic immunity. The Inspector radioed for police help, and soon the truck was brought to the Ostia police station.

At Ostia, the police commissioner assumed command, in consultation with the Inspector, and they broke open the diplomatic seals and lifted the lid of the big trunk.

Hardened policemen who had seen everything, or nearly everything, gasped at the grotesque contents of the trunk. A helmeted man was squeezed in the padded trunk. He was seated on a small, low stool. His nose pressed against his knees, his mouth was gagged, his hands were tied behind his back. He wore slacks and a shirt; his sockless feet were strapped in yellow slippers which were screwd tight to the floor of the trunk. The heat inside the trunk was unbearable. Ventilation came through four small holes in the lid of the trunk. The sickening smell of anesthetic wafted up from the open trunk. This was a diplomatic pouch specially designed to transport human beings. Shoulder pads and a padded cushion protected the man's body and spine from bumps. An abdominal strap held him in a fixed position, reinforced by a tangle of straps and ropes after the fashion of ancient mummies.

Judging from the wear and tear, both inside and outside the trunk, and perspiration stains on the cushions and lining, the police officers concluded that this "Diplomatic Pouch" had delivered many reluctant passengers to undesired destinations.

The man in the trunk was released from his harness; as he tried to stretch his cramped arms and legs, he fainted. Revived, he showed signs of having been drugged. Delirious, he vomited and had to lie down.

When the man in the trunk recovered from the drugs and the effect of his bonds, he was happy to talk to his liberators. Transferred to headquarters in Rome, he identified himself as Joseph Dahan, born March 5, 1934 in Oujda, Morocco, and now a citizen of Israel. He was carrying a Moroccan passport, dated 1961 and issued in Damascus. This aroused the suspicions of his interrogators. They wondered about the story being unfolded by the "Man in the Trunk."

Dahan said he had arrived in Rome a few days ago and was sitting in the Cafe de Paris on Via Veneto when he was spotted by three Egyptian Embassy officials seated nearby. He had been working as an interpreter for the U.A.R. Embassy. The Egyptians joined Dahan and plied him with drinks. When Dahan got drunk, he was led out by his convivial companions to their car. He woke up in a villa somewhere in the country, he had no idea where. He felt drugged and lost consciousness. The next thing he knew he was trussed in a tight place. Gagged, he succeeded in loosening the tape around his mouth, and shouted for help. This was the muffled cry heard by the porter and the Inspector at the airport.

Why was he kidnapped for a trip in a trunk to Cairo?

"Since I was an interpreter for the Egyptian Embassy, they figured that I had learned too much about their supply deals with Italy and other countries for arms. They must have thought I would pass on this information, selling it to other Intelligence Services. In my work I learned something about the Egyptians' Intelligence, and also about their political subversion in other countries. So, believing I knew too much and was too dangerous, they decided to get rid of me, and take me to Egypt. This is what I figured out. Nobody told me anything, or tipped me off."

The Rome investigators were not convinced and pressed Dahan to clear up doubts and contradictions.

Their first look at Dahan made the police distrust him. His hair was dyed blonde.

He was confused by the police interrogation. Did he come to Rome from Naples? And why did he live under an assumed name in Naples? What was he doing in Frankfurt? Where did he get a large sum of money that he claimed to have brought to Rome? For what service was he paid the money? What secret information had he acquired at the Embassy? Was this really the reason for his trunk ride?

Checking around Embassy Row in Rome, the police learned only that nobody knew about him. The Moroccan Embassy diplomatically knew nothing and would not intervene for a man who said he was born in Morocco. The Israel Embassy had no record of a man named Joseph Dahan. The Syrian Embassy records did not show a passport issued to Joseph Dahan.

The day after the trunk discovery, a Rome newspaper published a sensational story that Joseph Dahan was "a dangerous double agent, perhaps a triple agent, serving Egyptian Intelligence, selling U.A.R. secrets to Israel, and informing NATO about secret deals with both Middle East protagonists."

Sensation followed sensation in the Rome press, with the wire services relaying every detail around the world. The Italian Foreign Ministry ordered the expulsion of the two Egyptian Embassy officials who attempted to send the "Man in the Trunk" to Cairo. The Ministry identified them as First Secretaries Abdel Mosein El Neglawy and Salim Osman el Sayed, and informed them they were to leave Italy within twenty four hours. Their expulsion was vigorously protested by U.A.R. Ambassador Ahmed Naguib Nashin in a personal appearance at the Italian Foreign Ministry. Nashin's protest was firmly rejected by Count Guerino Roberto, Chief of Protocol.

The Egyptian Ambassador aroused the ire of the

Foreign Ministry and the Rome press by openly charging in his note that the Italian police replaced the Egyptian "Diplomatic Pouch" with another trunk containing the Israeli spy, Joseph Dahan.

Nicolas Soire, Chief of Rome's Police Motorized Brigade, informed reporters that "Italian counter-espionage has taken the trunk affair in hand. One thing we are certain of — Joseph Dahan is not Joseph Dahan."

The news service telex machines clattered out the bulletin from Jerusalem: "Joseph Dahan's real name is Mordecai Ben Massoud Luk, born 1935, in Spanish Morocco, emigrated to Israel in 1949, married in Israel, father of four children living with their mother in Petah Tikvah, where he was a carpenter, when last seen there in 1953." Luk had served in the Israel Army. Then he turned to a life of crime. He participated in armed robberies and was sentenced to a thirty month prison sentence. Israeli and Italian police compared fingerprints and verified Dahan-Luk's true identity. Israel authorities accused Luk of serving as a spy for Egypt and denied any connection between Luk and Israeli Intelligence. Israeli authorities were considering requesting extradition of Luk.

Newspapers in Rome and throughout Europe and Britain had a field day, speculating on all the angles, incredible as some may appear, of the "Man in the Trunk."

A Paris paper featured a questionable story from Beirut that President Nasser had taken a personal interest in the investigation of the trunk affair.Nasser was reported to have burst into a rage when he learned that Luk had been injected with a shot of morphine instead of being drugged for a longer period to keep him quiet until he reached Cairo. The Beirut dispatch linked Luk with the bomb threats that harried the German scientists working on the development of Egyptian missiles and planes.

Another Paris journal presented conflicting theories advanced to explain the "Man in the Trunk" mystery. One supposition pictured Luk as a deserter from the Israeli Army who found refuge in Egypt where he was trained to be a small-time spy in the pay of Cairo. An opposing explanation was that Luk had been working for Israeli Intelligence, assigned to spy on and sabotage the Egyptian missile project. His trip to Germany was connected with the ex-Nazi scientists hired by the Nasser regime.

A Rome commentator figured out that Luk's job for Israel Intelligence was to follow the spy networks of other European and Mediterranean powers from the vantage point of the Italian capital. Other Israeli secret agents had disappeared in Italy. They had either been kidnapped or mysteriously eliminated by enemies of Jerusalem, according to this commentator. He played up the idea that the trunk was a regular method for kidnapping people on Cairo's wanted list.

In Tel Aviv, *Yediot Achronot* interviewed Luk's wife, Nurit. His 29-year-old wife (whom he had deserted eleven year earlier) considered herself as separated.

"I want him brought back to Israel for one purpose, so I can get divorced from him," said Nurit Luk who called her estranged husband "an adventurer, a wanderer, a no-good who runs away and doesn't support his four children."

Luk's mother-in-law was harsher in talking to *Yediot Achronot*. "A lazy rascal," she shouted. "He'd rather go dancing than work."

Even Luk's mother and father felt they were disgraced by their son, and disowned him. However, former neighbors, had a good word for Luk as a capable carpenter and an interesting conversationalist.

Paris Jour heated up the story with a Rome dispatch saying that Luk was by no means a third-rate secret agent. Diplomatic circles in Rome believed Luk was a very important Israeli agent who had penetrated Egyptian Intelligence. *Paris Jour* stated that the Tel Aviv stories about Luk's philandering and absenteeism were cover-ups for his serious business as an Israeli Intelligence agent.

Italian police, suspecting that the Luk case was not the only use of the trunk for human transport, checked out every tip and angle. Detectives were placed around the Egyptian Embassy to report on comings and goings of diplomatic officials and others with business there. A squad of other detectives reconstructed the Luk episode at the airport and concluded that others also were implicated in the attempted kidnapping. Youssef Ahmed Khalter and Abdel Salem were suspected, and since they never were listed on the registry of the U.A.R. Embassy, they were not protected by diplomatic immunity.

Salem was picked up. It was learned that he actually was a secretary of the U.A.R. Embassy, although not officially listed. He was declared persona non grata and expelled from the country on an early flight to Cairo. Khalter vanished without a trace.

Investigation of Luk's background revealed that at least four women were involved with him in Naples. Sara Bianco, a 24-year-old curvaceous brunette, lived in the same house with Luk. She was the niece of the landlord. Sara professed her undying love for Mordecai and was convinced that he would fulfill his promises to marry her. When she was told by the detectives that Luk was married and had a wife and four children in the State of Israel, she collapsed in a shrill outburst of broken-hearted remorse. But when she was revived, she said she still loved Mordecai and would help pay for a lawyer to defend her lover. When Luk heard this, he refused to accept her help.

Dora Mosca, a 32-year-old Neapolitan legal secretary, told investigators that she met Luk casually on the street after each had noticed the other passing by. They thought it was "love at first sight" and spent many hours together in the days that followed. Luk proposed to Dora and she happily consented but thought he ought to ask her father for his daughter's hand, in the Italian tradition. Mr. Mosca, wiser than his daughter in the ways of non-Neapolitan strangers, invited Luk to show the prospective father-in-law his passport. Luk said he would bring it the next day. Neither saw Mordecai Luk again.

Luk moved to a modest hotel and played upon the sympathies of the elderly landlady to let him pay less than the other tenants. She was fond of her young cavalier who brought her images of Catholic saints and repeatedly told her how he admired her grace and charm.

"He was so poor, so sweet and so considerate. I loved him," the landlady told the police investigators.

His fourth fiancee, Edith Domula, seemed to have been a 19-year-old German blonde beauty.

NATO officers stationed in Rome knew about Edith but none could cast any light on her connections with Luk. The Italian detectives could not trace her whereabouts.

Searching Luk's room in Naples, detectives found an abundance of well-tailored suits, expensive shoes and shirts, and some unusual objects. A large signet ring shone with an engraved dragon. Playing with the ring, an officer unexpectedly sprung open the dragon to expose an empty hole in which microfilm or poison could be concealed.

Interpol cooperated in the investigation, but its inquiries in Germany, Switzerland and Poland yielded only unproductive indications that Luk had visited Frankfurt, Munich and Basel several times.

Luk was not very helpful, sticking to his unadorned story that he had worked for the Egyptian Embassy in Rome as a translator.

In the course of his duties as translator, Luk added that he would travel to Germany and Switzerland to take on additional duties of acquiring information for U.A.R. Intelligence. In Naples, he was asked to keep track of other foreign agents from other countries.

Italian counter-espionage officials were convinced at this point that Luk was an Israeli who had betrayed his country to work for Egyptian intelligence, and finally fell out with his Arab employers who were determined to get him out of the way and dispose of him in Egypt. Investigation so far had not uncovered anything to indicate that Luk had harmed the interests of Italy. Therefore, the Italian Government expressed no opposition to Jerusalem's request for extradition, particularly in view of Luk's willingness to be returned to Israel. He told the Israel Embassy representative that he wanted to be repatriated to Israel to escape revenge by the Egyptians who would be angry at his narrow escape from the trunk. The Israel Embassy official promised Luk nothing more than that he would face prosecution by a court of law in Israel.

"Anything is better than to fall into the hands of the Egyptians now," replied Luk. "Israel is the only safe place where they can't get at me." Luk requested one favor that he be permitted to make a public statement thanking the Italians for their kind treatment.

A press statement was released under his name in which he thanked the Italian people for their hospitality and the police for saving his life. "I want to say that I acted wrongly to my own country and to my wife and children. When I will have expiated my errors, I hope to start a new life with my family. I am a carpenter. It is the only trade in which I want to work," his statement concluded.

Figaro commented, "Some see in Luk's farewell statement and his return to his homeland the proof that he was in fact an Israel Secret Service agent."

Luk was escorted on the El Al flight to Lydda by an

Israeli Embassy official. As soon as he set foot on the soil of his own country, Israeli police stepped forward to arrest him.

A *France-Soir* correspondent made a reservation on the same flight and wangled an interview out of Luk. "While I was locked up in the trunk, I kept telling myself I must get out of this," *France-Soir* reported on the conversation with Luk, "So many men have been sent to Cairo this way. But I'll get out of it. As you see, I did. I'm happy to be returning to Israel. After all, I never worked against my country. I have now rendered Israel a great service. The Egyptian Intelligence Services in Europe are now unmasked. I know how they function, who belongs to them, and I shall give this information to our people in Israel. I have had six months training in espionage with two Egyptian experts. I am sure that the courts in Israel will understand this and let me go free."

The trial of Mordecai Luk in May 1965 deflated the trunk incident to minor proportions. The story of Luk's unlucky life was pieced together from his confessions to the police and the court, and additional information volunteered by his family.

Israeli police records showed four arrests, including armed robbery. He disappeared from the country in 1953 while on army reservist training near the Gaza Strip. Crossing the armistice line, he lost himself in Gaza, posing as an Arabic-speaking native of Morocco. Egyptian Army officers in Gaza welcomed an escapee from Israel as a potential spy, or informant, and arranged for his transfer to Cairo. Luk was imprisoned in Cairo as an enemy infiltrator. It soon developed that imprisonment was an Egyptian Intelligence way to soften him up for service to the U.A.R., if he was willing to cooperate.

Fluent in Arabic, Hebrew, English, French, Italian and German, Luk obviously was regarded as a find if he would collaborate willingly with the espionage service. Intelligence officers offered him freedom if he would speak on the Cairo Radio Hebrew program as an announcer of news broadcasts. Luk agreed to take the job and be released from prison. One day, his wife was listening to the Cairo Radio Hebrew program, and recognized her lost husband's voice. He was spewing out vicious anti-Israel propaganda and reporting wild exaggerations of non-existent Egyptian military successes over Israel in border incidents.

Israeli Intelligence, learning that Luk was speaking over Cairo Radio, put his name on a list. He was to be watched from then on. The radio-announcing job was considered to be the forerunner of more serious espionage assignments ahead for the fugitive from the Israel Army.

Before Luk's release from prison, he met other Israelis behind bars. They had slipped across the border into the Gaza Strip to escape prosecution in Israel for crimes and misdemeanors, to run away from family trouble, or to run away from themselves. A number of the Hebrew-speaking inmates were mental cases.

Mordecai, ever the ebullient extrovert, entertained his fellow inmates with songs of Israel, often interjecting secret messages for them in the lines he composed. The guards had little idea what the Israelis were up to.

Luk—Man in a Trunk

Until he was chosen as a candidate for radio announcer, the monotony of prison life overcame Luk's natural buoyancy, and he succumbed to fits of depression. Once, in a deep mood of despair, he slashed his wrists with a piece of metal loosened from his bedstead. He was saved by quick medical action and got some relief from prison tedium by spending a few days in the clinic. Back in his cell, and falling again into depression, Luk attempted suicide once more by prying the metal plate out of his heel and cutting his wrists again. This time, he lost a dangerous amount of blood, and the guards seemed tardy deliberately in calling the medical staff. Luk was a month in the prison hospital. During his confinement, he was visited by espionage officers who sounded him out for working for Egypt.

Luk pleaded for a chance to leave Egypt and strike new roots in Canada or the United States. He was placated with the promise of a hearing before an immigration commission. The hearing was a perfunctory formality which refused his plea. The espionage agents later hinted to Luk that "other arrangements might be made." They were impressed with his appearance and his linguistic talents, and considered him good material for espionage service.

Luk's imprisonment had indeed softened him up, and he was glad to win his freedom, first on the offer of the radio job, and afterwards, with willingness to train for espionage.

When Luk joined other recruits for espionage he found they included some Egyptian Jews and Israeli deserters and renegades. They learned how to handle themselves in various European environments. They were subjected to physical and psychological testing. From these psychological tests, the Egyptians learned that Luk, for one, was very fond of his children and missed them. He was subsequently warned that if he did not toe the line of obedience and discipline, then Egyptian agents in Israel would kill his children.

When Luk's training period ended in 1962, his immediate boss, known to him only as Mr. Said, told him, "You will soon go to Europe. According to the requirements of your mission, you will serve in France, Switzerland, Germany and Italy. Your first task will be to come into contact with Israeli citizens living in these countries. You will supply us with information about them. Find out about their professions, what they are doing abroad, what they know about internal affairs in Israel, what they think of the situation in Israel. You will be especially on the lookout for other secret agents. You will make contact with people in official positions."

Luk's starting salary was set at $150 a month. He was promised higher salaries depending on how well he carried out his duties. He was handed a passport with the name of Mohamed Hamdi Habal, and his own picture. A hair dyeing session changed Luk from a brunette to a blonde. Before being sent to Europe, he was flown to Damascus where he received a Moroccan passport under the name of Joseph Dahan.

This was an example of Egyptian-Syrian cooperation in the underworld of espionage, although the Arab brother nations were not beyond spying on each other.

During the next two years, 1962-1963, Luk lived and traveled under the name of Joseph Dahan, a Moroccan. He was busy working with Egyptian agents in recruiting German scientists for Nasser's military aircraft and missile projects. In pursuit of this recruiting program, he contacted scientific people in Munich, Coblenz, Frankfurt, Zurich and Basel.

On January 1, 1964, Luk-Dahan arrived in Naples and settled down to a less glamorous existence. Without his travel allowance, he had to scrimp on his $150 a month salary, which had remained unchanged. Accustomed to the good life on a travel expense account, and having a weakness for feminine pulchritude, the dashing young Moroccan known as Joseph Dahan felt frustrated in Naples for lack of funds. He tried to supplement his meager pay by taking on some extra work as a tourist guide, but this was only an infrequent accretion and he hated the indignity of tips.

Lacking sufficient funds to enjoy the life to which he had become accustomed, Dahan had to lower his living standards. He found a cheap boarding house operated by an elderly landlady. Bored and unhappy, strapped for funds, and feeling guilty about lining up German missile and aircraft scientists for research aimed at the destruction of Israel, Dahan decided to force the issue with his employers for more money.

The next time he was scheduled to meet with "Mr. Said," who was First Secretary of the Egyptian Embassy, he raised the matter of a salary increase.

185

"More money!" El Sayad, alias "Mr. Said," challenged Dahan. "You are not even worth what we pay you. What you give us in information isn't worth a piaster."

Dahan retorted that unless he got more money, he would defect to the Israelis who would pay more money.

What happened following this argument was foggy in Luk-Dahan's mind. The next thing he could remember was waking up in the claustrophobic blackness of the trunk, yelling for help.

Returning to Israel of his own free will on November 24, 1964, Luk faced charges of serving the enemy, and dealing with Intelligence for an enemy of the State. He went on trial May 17, 1965 in the Jerusalem District Court. He entered the courtroom neatly dressed, wearing dark glasses. Appearing confident, he passed the word to a newspaper reporter that he was sure he would get off with a light sentence.

The President of the District Court ordered the trial to be held in camera, with the press and public barred from the courtroom as soon as it became evident that Israel Secret Service had been watching Luk's movements from the time he disappeared in 1953 until he reappeared in European cities and contacted Israeli travelers and representatives of commercial and institutional bodies abroad.

Luk categorically denied the charges that he served the Egyptians.

On September 10, the Jerusalem Court declared Mordecai Luk guilty of establishing a close relationship with

Egyptian Intelligence in activities which harmed the security of the State of Israel. The Court rejected the argument of the defense that the attempted trunk abduction proved that Luk in fact was working against Egypt. The Attorney General argued for imposition of the maximum penalty, life imprisonment. The Court handed down a 13-year-prison sentence.

Now, some five years after the dust has settled on the drama of the "Man in the Trunk," it can be revealed that Luk was saved from the trunk not by sheer luck, but by his own country's alert counter-espionage work. The Israeli agents learned of the plan to kidnap Luk. The Israeli agents tipped off the Italian authorities in time, and the airport customs officials were ready for the trunk.

Israeli Intelligence, regarded as one of the best, if not the sharpest in the world, have a high opinion of their Italian counterparts. Cooperation between the two services blocked the "Man in the Trunk" from reaching his Cairo destination and an unknown fate.

CHAPTER TWELVE

NASSER'S NETWORK

Mordecai Luk was not the first "Man in the Trunk" but he was fortunate to be the only known occupant of the "Diplomatic Pouch" to be rescued en route to Cairo.

The "Man in the Trunk" case aroused world attention to the unorthodox methods of President Nasser's Secret Services. What was not known was the magnitude and extent of the Egyptian spy network, which is counted in underground circles to be the fifth largest in the world.

Known in Arabic as Moukhaberat, the Egyptian Secret Services were organized by Nasser himself when he was Minister of Interior, prior to his accession to power in 1952.

Moukhaberat is organized in four main departments. First and most important is Intelligence, which includes subdivisions for documentation, political propaganda, subversion and foreign political activities. A Special Secret Service headed by Hassan el Aish was established within Intelligence in 1960 to execute operations abroad such as trunk kidnappings, assassination, and subversion. General Salah Nasser directed Intelligence until he was sacked for his failures in misleading Abdul Nasser and his generals to trigger the Six Day War. Salah Nasser was one of Nasser's scapegoats for the June 1967 disaster that befell Egypt.

Next in priority is the department of Military Intelligence. Egyptian military attaches in overseas embassies, all enjoying diplomatic immunity, serve Military Intelligence.

The third department is Internal Security. The former chief of Internal Security, Mohammed Khalifa, was fired in 1966 for overlooking the creation of a united anti-Nasser plot between the Moslem Brotherhood and dissident army officers until virtually the eleventh hour before the scheduling of the coup.

The fourth department directly served President Nasser and reported straight to Nasser carrying out his personal requests. Nasser, however, arranged for all four department heads to contact him personally whenever they had confidential information for the President.

Many Egyptian operatives abroad are associated with embassies, directly or indirectly, so they will be covered by diplomatic immunity. Other U.A.R. agents operate under other semi-official covers. The Egyptian El Masr Import-Export Company has branches all over the world, and its swollen payroll is replete with secret service men masquerading as commercial agents. United Arab Airlines also has an extraordinarily large staff at downtown offices and airports, many never showing up at airline jobs but using the airline as a cover for spying. Middle East News Agency, MENA, assigns "correspondents" and editors in

189

places where the Associated Press would not deem it newsworthy to have even a stringer. Acting as foreign correspondents, accredited MENA staff members gained access into highest circles of foreign governments, industries, armies and other "sacred" places to wheedle information for Cairo headquarters.

Said Mutahir, regional director in Ethiopia for United Arab Airlines, served on the side as contact for the Eritrean Liberation Movement dedicated to the overthrow of the Ethiopian royal family.

Egyptian "diplomats" all over the globe probably hold the world's record for being kicked out of their assigned countries as "persona non grata."

At least eighteen nations in the past two decades expelled Egyptian Embassy officials, airline, commercial and MENA representatives for espionage or subversion.

The Congo kicked out the entire staff of the Egyptian Embassy, headed by the Ambassador, in 1960 for aiding the Congolese rebels. Ghana and Guinea closed down the cultural departments of the Egyptian Embassies for subversive programming far removed from culture.

Arab brotherhood could not disguise the subversive activities of Egyptian agents in Saudi Arabia and the Sudan where President Nasser sought to spread his hegemony even at the attempted sacrifice of his fellow Moslem rulers. The Egyptian Special Secret Services were accused of having their hands in assassinations and attempted assassinations in Iraq, Jordan, Tunisia and Lebanon. Repeated assassination attempts against Jordan's King Hussein and Tunisia's President Bourguiba were linked with

U.A.R. emissaries. They hit their mark in the murder of Jordanian Prime Minister Hassan Madjali, and again in the mysterious slaying of an anti-Nasser Beirut journalist, Kamil Mrowa.

Egyptian secret agents were especially numerous in such strategic cities as New York, Geneva, Zurich, Munich, Frankfurt, Buenos Aires, Beirut, Dakar, Nairobi and Brazzaville, as well as all European capitals.

From 1960 until the 1967 War, Rome was the center of Egyptian espionage in Western Europe. When General de Gaulle switched French policy from pro-Israel to pro-Arab during the 1967 Israel-Arab War, Paris supplanted Rome as the heart of the Egyptian underground operation.

In Egyptian Embassies, the First Secretary served as Chief of Secret Service and Intelligence. The First Secretary usually undercut the authority of the Egyptian Ambassador, and often issued orders to him. Salim Osman el Sayad, First Secretary of the Egyptian Embassy in Rome, engineered the "Man in the Trunk" operation and was expelled the day after the discovery of the prisoner in the "Diplomatic Pouch." It developed that the trunk affair was planned and carried out without the knowledge of the Ambassador.

During the years of Egypt's estrangement from France, from the 1956 Sinai War to the 1967 Six Day War, the decade in which the U.A.R. Paris Embassy was closed, Rome grew in importance as the fulcrum of Cairo's overseas network. Out of Rome, the United Arab Airlines flew secret agents on missions through Europe,

Africa, Asia, North and South America. Italian cities swarmed with Egyptian travel agencies, airline and commercial firms.

Many of the Egyptian commercial companies fronted for armaments purchases and deliveries from many producing countries and shipment throughout the Arab world. Egyptian tourist agencies were conduits for recruiting and sending mercenaries to fight in African revolts.

The trunk was a specific Egyptian travel feature, reserved for the doomed. Sharif Shaker, a former Egyptian Intelligence agent who defected, revealed that the trunk conveyed two U.A.R. anti-Nasser plotters from Europe to Cairo for torture and execution. Shaker said the trunk was designed by a German technician, one Helmut Herbinger, an S.S. Colonel during the Nazi period. Trunks were posted from Bonn and Beirut for delivery with human cargo to Cairo. In January 1964, Egyptian Army Lieutenant Colonel Nabil Metwayi disappeared from his residence in Beirut. An opponent of Nasser, he fled Egypt and obtained political asylum in Lebanon in 1963. The last time he was seen he was being accompanied by two strangers near his home. He was drugged, crammed into a trunk, and delivered to Cairo for certain execution. In 1962, a trunk from Bonn carried off Dr. Heinz Krug, German expert on missile fuel, who was suspected of supplying his know-how to Israel. Dr. Krug's associate at the Institute of Space Research in Stuttgart, Professor Sanger, lost his position after he was exposed for preparing missile projects for Cairo.

An ultra-secret Branch of The Egyptian Special Secret Service was called Service-Action. This branch specialized in probing anti-Nasser plots.

Colonel Ramadan, U.A.R. military attache at the Embassy in Bonn, was recalled to Cairo for consultation. On his arrival, Colonel Ramadan was arrested for organizing a plot against Nasser's life. One of the key plotters was the Egyptian military attache in Damascus, Colonel Zagloul Abdul Rahman. He outsmarted Service-Action. When he was summoned back to Cairo at the same time as Ramadan, he sensed danger and took the next plane out of Damascus for Beirut. He lives in anonymity in Switzerland.

In 1964, an Egyptian Air Force pilot surprised the world by defecting and flying his MIG fighter plane to an Israeli airport. The Israelis rolled out the red carpet for their unexpected guest, treated him royally, took him on tours of the country so he could see for himself what the Jews had done to make the desert blossom. The Israeli Intelligence quietly arranged for the Egyptian pilot to settle down comfortably in Argentina, with a new identity, a neutral passport, and a well-paying job in civil aviation.

Soon after the Egyptian flyer arrived in Buenos Aires, via Paris, he disappeared. It was believed that he was tracked down by a woman operative of Service-Action and forcibly taken aboard a United Arab Airliner for return to Cairo. The runaway pilot was tried for high treason, found guilty and summarily executed in July, 1964.

A German physicist, Dr. Hans Ehrhardt, who had taught for a time at Egypt's Ibrahim Pasha University on the Faculty of Electronics, communicated with U.A.R. authorities that he had invented a secret weapon, ultra short wave shock cannon. It was like something out of science fiction. He was granted a research fund and flew to Cairo to work on his fantastic project. In 1968, he said he had to return to Munich where facilities existed for testing the outlandish cannon.

Dr. Ehrhardt, under pressure, informed his employers of the precise location of the field tests, at an isolated lake in Bavaria. What happened next to Dr. Ehrhardt is guess work. Was he suspected by Service-Action of bluffing, or selling out his invention to the Israelis?

While on his Munich trip, he was invited by a Service-Action envoy to have a beer in a Munich beer hall. The inventor passed out, and lay for four days between life and death in a Munich hospital. Physicians ordered laboratory tests and discovered that he had traces of a powerful poison in his blood. The poison was Sacharan, manufactured in Egypt.

Counter-espionage agents who respect the achievements of Service-Action say its operatives like to perform with James Bond daring. "They read too many spy stories and take the James Bond movies too seriously," remarked a French counter-espionage agent. "And they talk too much."

The Frenchman passed us a clipping from the *Herald Tribune,* published in Paris on May 25, 1968. It read: "A gang of six professional killers was reported to have left Cairo for Tunis on a mission aimed at assassinating President Bourguiba. Traveling in pairs, the would-be assassins planned to come by way of Vienna. All six are rated as first class marksmen and specialists in explosives. Their cover assignment was "advisers to Middle East arms dealers." Tunisian security forces, forewarned of the killers' arrival, took measures to protect President Bourguiba."

The Frenchman smiled, "You see Bourguiba has nine lives."

CHAPTER THIRTEEN

THE ODD CITIZEN

A rather odd citizen of Israel lived in the asbestos hut No. 689, on Street No. 1, located in a poor quarter of Ashkelon, a town seven kilometers from Egyptian-held Gaza. The modest hut was the "operational basis" of an Egyptian citizen of Armenian origin, Kozyak Yakubian, who was in fact an Egyptian agent. On his door, one could read, scribbled in large letters, the name he went by in Israel: Yitzhak (Jacques) Kutchok — a Jewish immigrant who came from Brazil under the auspices of the Jewish Agency.

For one year after his arrival Yakubian, alias Kutchok, had followed an intensive Hebrew course in an *Ulpan* in Kibbutz Negba. He had then worked as a truck driver in Israel's army, and once his military service was completed, he had received from the Jewish Agency a modest home in Ashkelon.

Neither he nor his chiefs realized that Yakubian had been under constant surveillance since January 1962, about a month after his arrival, by Israeli counter-espionage, the Shin Bet (the word is made up of the first letters of the two Hebrew words, Sherut Bitachon, meaning Security Services).

Having spotted the spy even before he began operations, the Security Services kept an eye on him, in order to track down other Egyptian agents, and perhaps dismantle their network.

As it turned out the Security Services were obliged, for very human reasons, to arrest him prematurely. The spy had fallen in love with a young girl from Negba, and the Services had to intervene to prevent them from getting married. The young girl knew nothing about Yakubian's real identity, and the girl's parents had already consented to their marriage.

Arrested in his hut, Yakubian cooperated with the police, showing them the hiding place in his room where he kept all the equipment needed by a second-rate spy. The door was sealed.

The young girl, who knew nothing, arrived a few hours later, directly from the army unit in which she served, only to learn that the man she was to marry was an Egyptian spy.

Yakubian gave the detectives a detailed account of the route which he had followed to reach Israel. An extraordinary itinerant photographer, he had joined the Egyptian Secret Services in 1959. His training had lasted over a year, during which he was given to read an impressive number of books and magazines dealing with the economy, politics and army of Israel. He was taught topography, and coding, how to use invisible inks and handle a transmitting post. He was able to show the Israeli in-

197

vestigators that long before he had served in Israel's army, he knew the exact location of many military camps and other places out of bounds to civilians.

In order to pass as a Jew, he underwent circumcision, a painful operation for a mature man. Then he regularly attended services in Cairo's main synagogue, in order to familiarize himself with Jewish rites. Finally, the Egyptian Security Services provided him with an identity card in the name of Yitzhak Kutchok, born in Turkey in 1935. (He was actually born in 1938).

Following his chiefs' instructions, late in 1960, he applied to the U.N. office in Cairo, and on the pretext that the local authorities had refused to renew his residence permit, he requested a refugee identity card, which he obtained on October 26, 1960. With this document, which indicated he was a Turkish refugee in Egypt, he applied for an immigration visa to Brazil, and left Egypt on March 1961.

He reached Rio de Janeiro on April 26. An Egyptian Secret Service man, who posed as the representative in Brazil of the Egyptian Bureau of Commerce, awaited him in Rio, and ordered him to go to Sao Paulo. There, another Egyptian provided him with a Brazilian identity card in the name of Kutchok, a Brazilian citizen of Jewish faith. With this new identity card, he returned to Rio, where he found work as a photographer.

A few months later, in the fall of 1961, Kutchok presented himself to the Jewish Agency office in Rio, declared his intention of emigrating to Israel, and demanded that the help extended to all new immigrants who could not pay their passage be accorded to him.

The Jewish Agency, the executive branch of the Zionist movement, thus approved the application of the Egyptian spy. On December 21, 1961, Kutchok landed in Haifa aboard the *Possa*. The Israeli authorities furnished him with an immigrant card bearing the number 180 598; his identity card indicated that he was of Turkish origin and came from Brazil.

On his way, Kutchok had stopped off in Genoa for a week, in order to meet one of his chiefs from Cairo, and receive his latest instructions. He was asked to do all he could to enter the Israeli army, preferably in a tank unit.

After an untroubled year, during which he learned the rudiments of Hebrew, Kutchok was called up. But he did not succeed in being admitted to the tank unit; counter-espionage, following his trail, had tracked down others who had been planted by Egypt, and had advised the Army not to entrust him with a job more responsible than that of truck driver.

Yakubian was bored, and did not succeed in gathering the information he knew Cairo would sooner or later require of him. To the great astonishment of his fiancee, who was herself in the Army, he demanded to be released exactly a year after his induction.

Then, with the help of the Jewish Agency, he settled in Ashkelon, where he shared a two-room hut with another immigrant, Albert Amiel. But neither his companion, nor any other neighbor ever entered the spy's room, although Kutchok was constantly attempting to make friends with the young men in the neighborhood.

Having vainly attempted to find work as a photographer, up to the time of his arrest he had never paid his modest rent amounting to IL. 18 monthly (about $ 6) to the building company, Amidar. Under the circumstances, no one in Ashkelon suspected that "poor Kutchok" was an Egyptian spy. True, he spoke fluent English, French, Arabic and Portuguese, but then, what Jew does not speak half a dozen languages?

Yakubian, alias Kutchok, was arrested before making a mess of the life of the young girl from Negba. He was tried in Jerusalem, and sentenced to life imprisonment.

Once the judgment was passed, he asked for only one favor: permission to wear in prison the judo "black belt" he had won during his period of training with Egyptian Secret Services!

CHAPTER FOURTEEN

NASSER FINANCES THE NEGEV'S DEVELOPMENT

A certain textile plant in Kiryat Gat, located in the heart of the Negev, exported fabrics to Paris and London. But its secret function was to provide a home for Egyptian spies, infiltrated into Israel under the guise of textile experts.

This clever Egyptian plan was actually never put into practice. It was revealed in all its details in the course of a trial which ended in Jerusalem in 1965.

The "star" of the trial was an industrialist living in Israel, who possessed French citizenship, Samuel (Sammy) Barukh. He was sentenced to eighteen years in jail for espionage.

How could the son of an honorable family, who had settled in Jerusalem four generations back, reach the point where he could serve the enemy and betray the country of his parents?

"Samuel Barukh fell victim to his unquenchable thirst for money, to which were added feelings of frustration, disappointment, and even hatred towards our country," the District Attorney stated.

Why did the crafty Egyptians' plan fail?

"It failed because of Samuel Barukh himself. He never had the slightest intention of really putting it into practice, although he had agreed to do so," the Defense Attorney explained. "Quite the opposite," the Defense Attorney continued, "my client did all that was in his power to cause this plan to fail. Cairo kept asking him through different channels; what about our plans? Samuel Barukh always managed to avoid giving more than vague, noncommittal answers."

The trial was shortened considerably owing to the fact that Barukh (who looked much younger than his forty years) chose to plead guilty to three of the six charges of the indictment. Guilty of having established relations with the enemy to provide secret information, of having transmitted a certain amount of information concerning Israel's security, and finally, guilty of holding secret military information.

"I profoundly regret all I have done, but I can only repeat that I did not endanger the security of the State," Barukh declared in court.

The story of Barukh's treason was told by the District Attorney to the Court sitting in Jerusalem.

Samuel Barukh had built in 1960-61, a plant "Argadine" in Kiryat Gat. But soon after it began to function, he realized he was facing financial disaster. The high cost of labor, the mounting taxes and overhead costs, prevented his products from being competitive on the European market, while they could not find much of a market in Israel itself. All his efforts to cut down on the labor force and reduce overheads had little effect. After two years were up, he was practically broke.

"Barukh," the District Attorney stated, "felt that the State of Israel and its economic institutions were responsible for his failure. Bitter, frustrated, full of grudges, he reached the point where he was ready to do just anything in order to repair his fences.

"In September 1963, the accused went abroad, hoping to find the funds needed to get his business out of the red. He approached members of his family who lived in Geneva. But these relations refused to invest, having learned that the plant had just been closed by order of the Israeli Ministry of Finance. It was then that Barukh came into contact in Geneva with the emissaries of Egyptian Secret Services."

The Defense Attorney explained how Barukh had gotten in touch with the Egyptians. According to him, his own family in Geneva, seeing him so disraught, but unable to pull him out of his financial morass, suggested that he get in touch with a middle man, "a man who claimed he could provide Barukh with the necessary funds, to be provided by a country beyond the iron curtain."

The stranger came to the meeting Barukh's family had arranged; he was well aware of the financial position of the Israeli industrialist. He suggested accompanying Barukh "to a certain country where he would be provided with the needed funds." At this stage, Barukh claimed, he did not yet know the country in question was Egypt. But the misunderstanding—should matters have proceeded as the lawyer claimed—did not last long. Barukh accepted the stranger's offer, and a few days later he received an Egyptian passport bearing his name.

Barukh went to Egypt. During his four day visit, he met various Egyptian personalities, intelligence officers in particular. Their offer was simple but effective.

Cairo would supply him with the funds needed to get his factory operating, would pay all his debts, and would even help him sell his products in Europe. He would continue to be sole manager and owner of the enterprise. In exchange, he would only be required to play a passive role. He must allow his factory to function as the basis for Egyptian agents who would come to Israel under the guise of textile experts and technicians.

Barukh had a moment's hesitation. The Egyptians proved understanding.

"You needn't hurry," they told him.

They pointed out that they were not asking him to provide information on Israel. "We know more about it than you do," one of them joked. But before Barukh could make up his mind, he was taken around Cairo, touring and visiting the Pyramids, during which time his picture was taken, with characteristic Egyptian scenery in the background.

Barukh thus understood that his hosts had trapped him. He agreed to cooperate.

Having returned to Israel on October 20, 1963, Barukh kept in touch with Cairo through his Geneva contact for about a year. At least twice in the course of that year, he provided Egypt with useful information concerning Israel's security, always using the same method.

A hiding-place was provided in the metal binding of a prayer book which relatives or friends, ignorant of its contents, were merely to deposit at a certain address. In both instances, Barukh sent reports about the economic and military situation in Israel, mostly based on information culled from the local press, and various rumors. This was not really secret information. But his reports on economic matters, of which he was especially well informed, were certainly useful to Cairo.

Suddenly in 1964, Barukh seemed to have felt pangs of conscience. Instead of waiting for the promised funds, he sold all he owned, made various arrangements with his creditors, and decided to settle in Australia, after adopting a new name.

Barukh was flooded with letters from Geneva and Zurich, sent through various intermediaries, as the Egyptians put pressure on him. He did not answer, or else he sent evasive answers. Once he wrote to Zurich, announcing that he had changed his plans, intended entering the political arena in Israel and get himself elected to the *Knesset,* after which he would be of greater service to his friends.

Cairo did not let him go.

"The money is awaiting you in Switzerland," his Geneva intermediary wrote. But Barukh would not hear of it, and was busy preparing his emigration to Australia. A visa being difficult to obtain in Israel, he planned to leave for Europe, from where he would carry out the needed formalities. At that time he also received an interesting offer from a Brazilian industrialist, who offered him $ 2000 a month to work for him.

"My client was resolved not only to change his name, but to undergo facial surgery to change his features in order to escape from Egyptian Secret Services, which would have scoured Europe looking for him," the Defense Attorney stated.

But Samuel Barukh was not to leave for Europe. On November 25, 1964, at the moment of embarking in Haifa, he was arrested by the Security Services. They found in his suitcase clippings from various Israeli papers, and a report, written in English, on the economic situation in Israel, addressed to his intermediary in Geneva. The report also contained information on the Hawks the Americans were to supply to Israel, and a memorandum on a new type of tank (of Italian make, but which Barukh attributed to Israel's armaments industry).

He was sentenced to eighteen years in jail. Some papers judged this an unduly severe sentence. Those responsible for the country's security estimated that if the judgment was severe in relation to the information yielded to the enemy, it was in fact lenient, for matters could have gone far indeed. Furthermore, Barukh's case would serve as a warning to other Israeli citizens who at one time or another might need money.

In the cases of both Yakubian and Barukh while Israeli counter-espionage proved remarkably effective, the Egyptian Security Services proved that they have undoubtedly made great strides in comparison with the methods used by Nasser's "toughies" in the fifties.

PART IV

SHADOWS OVER EUROPE

CHAPTER FIFTEEN

SELF APPOINTED ZURICH SPY

Johann Neeser, born in Zurich in 1926, seemed destined to live the quiet, uneventful life of the neutral Swiss people. His mother was a native of Germany. His two older half-brothers, by his mother's first marriage, had served in the German Army. The Neeser family felt identified with the Nazi cause, and when World War II flared in 1939, Johann was 13 years old and like all European Christian youngsters admired the spectacular victories of the Luftwaffe and the Wehrmacht.

In 1942, Adolf Huber, Johann's half-brother, for some unknown reason ran afoul of the Nazi S.S., and he was interned in the Aschendorfermoor concentration camp.

As a German national, with another son in Hitler's military service, Frau Neeser succeeded in wrangling permission from Berlin to visit Adolf at Aschendorfermoor Camp. Johann, then 16, accompanied his mother on a trip that shaped his thinking forever afterwards. Having been reared in the undisturbed, harmonious, orderly, humane atmosphere of unwarlike Switzerland, young Johann was stunned to travel through the ruined city of Bremen, partially devastated by Allied bombing, and to see the ravages of war in the German countryside.

At the Nazi prison camp, he came face to face with his half-brother, a human skeleton, broken in body and spirit under Hitlerite torture and starvation. His mother's subsequent campaign to obtain Adolf's release failed, and they had to wait for the end of World War II before he could return home, an emaciated shell of a soldier.

The fleeting personal encounter with Nazism shattered the calm of this Swiss youth's charmed seclusion from the nightmare of war that visited the rest of Europe. He instinctively revolted against the cruelty and inhumanity of the Nazi regime, and wished for the defeat of Hitler, despite his family's German background. What caused the cultured German nation to sink to such depths? Asking himself this question, Johann read available books in the library on the subject of the rise of Hitlerism. He scanned the newspapers and magazines for articles about the Nazi mistreatment of the Jews, Poles and other victims of Hitlerian hatred. Not until the end of the war did the full story of the unspeakable extermination of the six million Jews of Europe come to light to nauseate an unbelieving world.

In April 1943, when the press highlighted the revolt of the Warsaw Ghetto Jews against Nazi shipments to the death camps, Johann saved every clipping and started a scrapbook on Nazi atrocities and the plight of the Jews. Many years later, in January 1960, he wrote to the International Red Cross and to the German and British Consulates in Zurich for unpublished documents relating to the details of the Warsaw Ghetto uprising and the Nazi extermination camps. Within weeks after making this request, he went to work early in 1960 in the photocopy department of the Zurich company, "M.T.P. Motoren, Turbinen und Pumpen. "M.T.P." operated as the official purchasing agent for the United Arab Republic, specializing in the procurement of industrial and agricultural machinery and raw materials.

Not until 1962 was it learned publicly that "M.T.P." was a front for the secret operations of an Egyptian multimillionaire, Hassan Sayed Kamil, a dashing jet set swinger in his early forties. Kamil broke into the headlines in July 1962, when he was cleared of suspicion of complicity in the death of his first wife, the Duchess Helen of Mecklenburg, in an airplane crash in Westphalia.

The plane accident led to investigation of Kamil's activities and he was revealed to be Nasser's agent in Zurich for the recruitment of German scientists and technicians for the Egyptian war industry. Kamil established the contact with the German Messerschmidt aircraft manufacturing firm which signed an agreement to provide Egypt with the prototype of a jet supersonic fighter-bomber aircraft capable of matching the Israel Mirage speed of Mach 2. Kamil also served as Middle East representative for Buehrle-Oerlikon, the great Swiss heavy industrial complex which produced air-to-ground missiles for the Egyptian warplanes.

Kamil organized a subsidiary of "M.T.P." under the name of MECO Mechanical Corporation which procured jet engines, aircraft spare parts and other equipment and raw materials for the warplane and missile factories operated by German scientists at Helwan, Egypt.

When Johann Neeser, a married man with three children, took a job with "M.T.P." in 1960, he had no idea of the company's farflung and secret operations.

He was soon to become privy to the secrets of "M. T.P." and "MECO." His job in the photocopy department gave him access to the plans, specifications, letters and documents that required extra copies. When he copied the lists of German scientists recruited by "M.T.P." and "MECO," he spotted the names of Nazi war criminals who escaped prosecution in the postwar trials.

As Neeser read the confidential material he was photocopying, he was fascinated by the intricate detail of the transactions between Cairo and Zurich, including the minutes of secret meetings of Egyptian, German and Swiss participants involved in building up Nasser's war machine.

Johann Neeser had never forgotten the torturing of his half-brother Adolf in Aschendorfermoor and he could never wipe out the horror of the Nazi slaughter of six million Jews, whose decimation he tabulated in his grim scrapbook of genocide.

As he followed the exciting story of the rise of the State of Israel and the gallant fight of the outnumbered Jews in Palestine to win their independence in the 1948 War, and their second victory over Egypt's Russian-supplied army in 1956, he gained a deeply held respect for the Jewish people, and admired what Jews accomplished in their homeland in Israel.

Self Appointed Zurich Spy

Johann, who had not a drop of Jewish blood in his veins, identified himself with the Jewish people in Israel. He inwardly rooted for their success and suffered when they suffered reverses and were threatened by their Arab enemies who constantly proclaimed that "the Jews must be driven into the sea."

Neeser had in his hands the photocopies of the secret plot of the Egyptian dictator Nasser to build the destructive weapons for a new war of annihilation of Israel, a "Second Holocaust" in his lifetime. He could not bear the thought of being a silent witness, and an indirect participant, in this hateful development toward a second genocide. He began to make extra photocopies to hide in his pockets or inside his shirt and take home after work.

A fellow employee caught him sneaking a photocopy into his coat pocket and informed the management's Security Services. One night in November 1961, there was a loud knock on the door of Neeser's apartment.

There stood his Boss, Hassan Kamil and Dr. Hans Lott, the company attorney who was a brother-in-law of Kamil.

"We've learned that you are hiding at home some of the documents that belong to our company," Kamil challenged Neeser.

The clerk in the photocopy department was overawed and overwhelmed by the appearance of the fabulous multimillionaire owner of the company, and afraid of the consequences of his theft of confidential documents. He readily admitted he had taken some documents home, and he agreed to produce them and return with them to the office with Kamil and Lott.

In the privacy of Kamil's office at night, the company owner and attorney put the pressure on the photocopy clerk. They cross-examined him and threatened him, trying to force out the reasons why he stole photocopies.

"I took documents home that were of technical interest so I could study them at my leisure," Neeser insisted.

"You stole our documents because you are working for Israeli Intelligence," Kamil thundered, "You are fired!"

Neeser trembled and protested that he had never been in contact with any Israelis. He did not know any Israelis. He had no intention of passing information to Israel.

Kamil and Lott conferred between themselves about the legal and publicity consequences of any police charges against Neeser and decided that they wanted to avoid any public exposure of the Company's dealings with Egypt. They better pay off Neeser and hope that the case would be forgotten. They informed Neeser that he would receive severance pay and he was never to enter the "M.T.P." offices again.

Worried about Neeser's future actions, Kamil said to him, "I hope you also will consider this miserable business closed. I'm not interested in pushing legal charges against you. I don't want any publicity. Do you realize what they would think of me in Cairo if they knew that one of my employees collected our confidential documents?"

"That's your problem, not mine," shouted Neeser as he regained his self-confidence. He jumped up from his chair, walked to the door, banged it closed, and strode away.

When Neeser returned to receive his severance pay, November 20, 1961, he was requested to sign an agreement that he would not transfer information or documents to any foreign person, company or country. The agreement specified that he must not accept any job or assignment from Israel, or any Israeli representative, for a three year period following the termination of his employment with "M.T.P."

After this incident, "M.T.P." instituted a policy which required all its employees to sign a similar document.

After his dismissal, Neeser found another job in Winterthur. Two years later, in March 1963, Hassan Kamil was back in the headlines.

The trial of Ben Gal and Jockelick, the Israeli agents who threatened the daughter of a German scientist working in Cairo, brought out the connections between the scientists and the "M.T.P." firm which recruited them. The Zurich newspaper *Blick,* on March 30, 1963 exposed Kamil's secret activities in a full page illustrated article, including copies of correspondence with Egyptian armaments factories.

At that point, Johann Neeser made up his mind to help the Israelis. He had hidden the photocopies in various closets and drawers and in his books in his apartment, and delivered only a portion of them to Kamil and

Lott on the night of their surprise visit. They had no idea how many photocopies Neeser had taken.

He wrote a letter to the Israel Army Intelligence in Tel Aviv, informing them that he had worked for "M. T.P." and had some valuable documents which might be helpful to Israel.

Two weeks later, Neeser received a reply, a typed, unsigned letter from Tel Aviv, informing him to proceed to London on March 24 and telephone the number enclosed. He was instructed to take all the documents in his possession. The letter said that a return airline ticket was reserved for him, and he should pick it up at the Zurich airline office.

On March 24, Neeser took the flight to London, carrying a hefty file of documents in a briefcase. The photocopies contained the delivery dates of jet engines and heavy equipment ordered by the F 135 and F 36 factories in Helwan.

But Neeser's lack of experience botched the mission.

At the London Airport, the British Passport Officer asks every incoming passenger: "How long do you intend to stay in Great Britain?" Neeser mumbled his answer: "Two or three days." The officer looked at Neeser's airline ticket, which was marked for a return flight to Zurich later the same day.

"Wait a moment," the officer instructed Neeser. He took Neeser's briefcase and vanished into another office. Twenty minutes later, the officer returned, summoned Neeser into the office, and asked him what he was doing with documents listing German, Swiss and Arab names, and including information about jet aircraft, engines, oil pumps, missiles and cooling systems.

Embarrassed, not knowing what to do, Neeser stammered, "These documents are of no value to me. You can throw them away."

"In that case, I'd rather confiscate them," the officer declared.

Upset, disgusted with himself for having fumbled his mission, and ashamed to call the number to admit that he lost the photocopies, Neeser sat around in the airport until time for the return flight and flew back dejected to Zurich.

He had taken only a portion of his voluminous file of photocopies to London, and he had retained duplicates of the documents that he lost in London.

The fate of Israel was uppermost in his mind and he determined to try again. He wrote to Israel Army Intelligence in Tel Aviv again, admitted the truth of how he mishandled the British Entry Officer and lost the documents, and offered to deliver another batch of photocopies.

Tel Aviv came right back with a prompt answer, arranged a new appointment, this time in Paris at the Hotel Normandie for April 6.

Neeser flew to Paris on the appointed date. A driver awaited him at a prescribed meeting place and drove him to the Place de Wagram. There a stranger accosted Neeser, saying, "Call me Peter or David, as you wish."

Peter-David asked Neeser for his file of documents and they adjourned to the Hotel Normandie to go over the contents. Neeser had catalogued his information:

1. A complete list of over a hundred internationally-known Swiss, German, English and Austrian companies selling military and nonmilitary equipment and materials to Egypt through "M.T.P." and "MECO." The companies included Buehrle-Oerlikon, S.I.G., Krupp, AEG, Kugelfischer, Ernst Leitz, Robert Bosch, Degussa, Deutsche Edelstahlwerke, Stahlunion-Export.

2. Minutes of a secret meeting held in Cairo between General Mahmoud Sidky, Chief of the Egyptian Air Force, who was deposed and imprisoned for U.A.R.'s air debacle June 5, 1967; Professor Messerschmidt; technical experts of the Egyptian aircraft industry, and Ferdinand Brandner, representative of Hassan Kamil.

3. Minutes of a confidential meeting between Kamil and top officials of Egyptian military and aircraft industries.

4. List of Egyptian orders for construction of the jet warplane HA—200, planned from the Messerschmidt prototype.

Examining the photocopies, Peter-David expressed satisfaction with Neeser's enterprise and told him that the information confirmed what Israeli Intelligence knew about Egyptian war production. He handed Neeser 350 francs for travel expenses, a reward of $ 100, and proposed that they meet again May 18 in Milan at the Americano Hotel.

Neeser, pleased with the success of his venture into

espionage for a cause in which he believed, offered to furnish a continuing flow of information. He had more documents at home, and he thought he could enlist one of his friends, still working in the copying department at "M.T.P.," to provide him with photocopies of current business.

When they met again in Milan, Neeser had completed a comprehensive research project based upon the material in his possession.

He presented Peter-David with a five page, single-spaced typewritten report detailing the following information:

The list of employees at "M.T.P.," with a personal sketch about each person's background, character traits, political opinions, and feelings toward Hassan Kamil.

A timetable of Kamil's working schedule and methods of operation.

"M.T.P." private code used in internal communications to camouflage delivery dates and the identification of war materials destined for Egypt.

Information concerning the scientists and technicians working in Cairo and Helwan.

A sketch about Brandner and a resume of his frequent trips between Zurich and Cairo. An opinion of qualified experts at "M.T.P." that Brandner was "an elephant in a China closet" instead of an aviation expert.

A description of the Helwan factory and research installations.

Lists of equipment and raw materials ordered for the Egyptian operation, 80 per cent of which already was installed at Helwan and Cairo.

Technical specifications of the jet engines for the HA—200 supersonic planes.

An account of the efforts of a Helwan engineer to purchase raw materials and equipment in the United States.

A recommended list of "M.T.P." employees who might be induced to cooperate with Neeser.

A report that Dr. Eisele, a physician in private practice in Cairo, visited Switzerland three times and Germany once. Dr. Eisele's daughter resided in Fribourg-en-Brisgau. Dr. Eisele attempted to contact Brandner, whose wife was a pharmacist, for the purpose of obtaining a steady supply of morphine. Brandner refused to collaborate with Dr. Eisele.

Peter-David's eyes widened when he read the report on Dr. Eisele. This was confirmation to Israeli Intelligence of the whereabouts of Dr. Hans Eisele, the Nazi doctor who conducted torturous medical experiments on Dachau concentration camp prisoners.

Dr. Eisele had been sentenced to death in absentia by the war crimes tribunal after World War II but escaped from Germany and found refuge in Egypt where he lived in a villa in the Cairo suburb of Maadi. He was medical adviser and physician to the German scientists and technicians working for Egyptian war industry.

In his report, Neeser described his friend, Wilhelm

Naf, who was in charge of the photocopy department at "M.T.P."

Naf, identified by Neeser by the code name of N.A., formerly served Kamil as his personal driver. In that capacity he took a lot of abuse from the highly-strung, temperamental Egyptian, and he vowed to avenge the indignities if he ever had an opportunity. When he confided his anger to Neeser, a plot was hatched to get even by turning over Egyptian secrets to Israel. Naf wanted money.

Peter-David smiled when he heard this. "We know about Naf already. Do you want me to give you Naf's address?" Peter-David thanked Neeser for his excellent, thorough-going report and his enthusiasm for the cause of Israel, handed him $ 35 for expenses and fixed a future appointment for June 15 in Paris. Neeser took Naf on his trip to Paris, and together they presented Peter-David with a sheaf of new documents on the latest developments at "M.T.P." To encourage Naf's participation, he was awarded $ 450. Supporting four daughters, Naf urgently needed money, and he was bought with the $ 450. They all agreed to meet again July 13 in Milan.

Peter-David's confirmation cable, "Will meet you as arranged," sent July 10 from London, did not reach Neeser's mail box. The cable was intercepted by Swiss police. At 1 a.m., July 9, 1963, Neeser was awakened by a visit from a Swiss police inspector, accompanied by Swiss security agents. He was arrested and hurried to police headquarters where he met Naf, who also was taken into custody. In the morning, Neeser and Naf were confronted by Kamil who formally accused the pair of stealing secret military information for the purpose of transmission to Israeli Intelligence in violation of Swiss laws and the neutrality of Switzerland.

At the hearing before a Zurich magistrate, Neeser pointed at his former employer and leveled the accusation: "Mr. Hassan Kamil, are you aware that President Nasser of Egypt is preparing with the assistance of your company the genocide of the Israeli people."

The magistrate, Judge Koeferli, ruled that Neeser's question should be stricken from the record.

The Defense Attorney, Dr. Manfred Kuhn, who had been hired for Neeser and Naf by "friends of the court," appealed to Judge Koeferli to dismiss the case on the grounds that the trial would reveal the traffic of war weapons and materials from Switzerland to Egypt, and the publicity of such revelations would harm the good name of the Swiss Nation and its neutral position.

Judge Koeferli denied Dr. Kuhn's plea and set the trial for May 8, 1964.

The trial in the Zurich District Court lasted only five hours. The indictment was watered down to the simple charge that Neeser and Naf had transmitted "intelligence of manufacturing secrets benefiting a foreign state and detrimental to a third state."

The Attorney General demanded sentences of 18 months imprisonment for Neeser and eight months for Naf, in addition to fines of 300 Swiss francs and 500 Swiss francs, respectively. The Defense Attorney, Dr. Kuhn, and his assistant Dr. Girsberger, concentrated on exposing the character of Hassan Kamil's business which surreptitiously violated Swiss neutrality by furnishing secret war materials to Egypt in its warfare with Israel.

Dr. Kuhn and Dr. Girsberger depicted Neeser and Naf as acting out of a sincere desire to help defend Israel against a power which sought to destroy the Jews of Israel. They acted out of sympathy for Israel, and not for money his argument went. Therefore, they should not be tried as professional espionage agents. Hassan Kamil chose the date of the trial to arrange business away from Zurich. The defense emphasized that Neeser was not recruited by a foreign power to spy, but volunteereed his services, and then enticed his friend Naf to help him.

Three days later, Judge Eugene Bosshard handed down his verdict. Neeser and Naf were judged guilty as charged, but let off with light sentences and token fines. It was obvious to court observers and to the press that the Swiss Government was anxious to play down the affair, minimize the publicity and finish the case with the least possible damage to the country's image of neutrality.

An unanswered mystery hung over the Neeser-Naf case. What part did British counter-espionage play in breaking up their supply of information to Israel? When Neeser was stopped by the British Entry Officer in London and surrendered his briefcase laden with "M.T.P." photocopies, he worried what would happen to the documents.

When he met Peter-David in Paris, he asked the Israeli agent, "What will the British do with my documents that they confiscated?"

"Don't worry. It's of no importance," Peter-David reassured the worried Neeser.

Four months later, in July 1964, Neeser was confronted by the same documents by Swiss detectives who interrogated him.

How did the photocopies find their way back to Zurich?

Did a British Entry Officer return them to Kamil for a price? Was this an undercover service of the British Government to the Swiss Government? Was this a cooperative gesture between the British and Swiss Secret Services?

Despite the public revelations, Kamil continued to operate his business without interference by the Swiss Government until 1968. Why? The Swiss had been pressing the Egyptian Government to pay compensation for nationalized and confiscated investments of Swiss citizens in Egypt, totaling 70 million Swiss francs. Kamil, serving as Nasser's agent in Zurich, was advising the Swiss Government on the handling of the Egyptian authorities on this restitution question.

Another reason for permitting Kamil's companies to operate unrestricted following the trial was the pressure exercised upon the Bern authorities by the Swiss industrial lobby, headed by Buehrle-Oerlikon, one of "M.T. P." 's chief suppliers. Buehrle-Oerlikon's representative in the Middle East was Mr. Hassan Kamil.

Kamil's financial honeymoon finally came to an ignominious end in 1968.

The Swiss press headlined Kamil's financial collapse

when he appeared in Zurich District Court and applied for bankruptcy proceedings for his "M.T.P." and "ME-CO" companies. Kamil explained his downfall as starting in 1965 when President Nasser called him to Cairo for urgent consultations. After being Nasser's man in Zurich for thirteen years, Kamil was curtly informed that he was finished. He had lost Nasser's trust.

Kamil became Nasser's scapegoat for the failures of Egypt's war industry. The Messerschmidt prototype HA—200 jet supersonic fighter-bomber which had to reach a speed of Mach 2 to match Israel's French Mirages never exceeded Mach 1.3. The ground-to-ground missile secretly assembled at Helwan never reached the operational stage. Many shipments of equipment and materials ordered from "M.T.P." never reached their destinations in Egypt, and other "M.T.P." shipments arrived late or in unsatisfactory condition. As a result of these failures, "M.T.P." was ordered by the Cairo Government to compensate it to the extent of 6 million Swiss francs. Kamil was forced to immediately deposit a bank draft to that amount. When Kamil returned to Zurich, he attempted to obtain a court order canceling the bank draft, arguing that the order was imposed under duress, but the Swiss Court refused his request.

The SF 6 million payment to Cairo forced Kamil's companies, "M.T.P." and "MECO" into bankruptcy. The Court ordered the liquidation of all of Kamil's business and personal properties in order to pay off creditors on a pro rata basis. Broken, bankrupt, Hassan Kamil's power, wealth, influence and glory suddenly ended in disorder and defeat. He disappeared from public view into oblivion.

A month after the "M.T.P." bankruptcy proceedings had vanished from the Swiss press, another international munitions affair flashed into the headlines.

The Federal Government of Switzerland accused directors of Buehrle-Oerlikon of a two-way violation of prohibitions against foreign armaments deals. The Swiss industrial giant was charged with illegal munitions traffic with both Egypt and Israel!

The Buehrle-Oerlikon case was followed up by still another Middle East affair involving strategic war weapons.

In September 1969, there burst into the open what *Schweizer Illustrierte* magazine called, "The most important espionage affair ever involving Switzerland."

German-born Hans Strecker, aged 32, employed by the Rotzinger Company near Basel, was caught stealing blueprints of thousands of parts of the French Mirage III-S fighter-bomber supersonic aircraft, the main striking force plane of the Israel Air Force in the Six Day War, and since then embargoed by the French regime. Intercepted redhanded as he packed cases of Mirage blueprints in his Mercedes car, Strecker said to the company official who stopped him, "I'm doing this with the agreement of the top management of our Company." Without further explanation, Strecker drove off towards the German frontier and was not seen in Switzerland again.

Tipped that the Mirage blueprints were headed for

Israel's Aircraft Industry, Swiss counter-espionage opened an investigation.

Suspicion centered on Alfred Frauenknecht of Aadorf, a department director at Winterthur Maschinefabric Gebrueder Sulzer AG, the aircraft company which was licensed to build the Mirage for the Swiss Air Force. Frauenknecht admitted to Swiss investigators that for a whole year he had been supplying Israeli agents in West Germany with scientific and technical data on construction of the Mirage. For this service, the Israelis had paid him SF 860,000.

In Tel Aviv, the Israel Defense Ministry spokesman had nothing to say to correspondents clamoring for confirmation or denial of the sensational Mirage story emanating from Switzerland.

The Swiss Government declared the Israeli military attache in Bern, Colonel Nehemia Kennan, persona non grata. Upon Colonel Kennan's return to Tel Aviv, he was appointed financial advisor to Army Chief-of-Staff, General Haim Bar Lev.

Ever since the Strecker disappearance with the Mirage blueprints, European journals periodically reported that the Israel aircraft industry was developing a "Super Mirage," Israel's own improved version of the Mirage which Paris had embargoed.

The Mirage, which had bested the Soviet-built MIG 21 in every aerial dogfight between Israeli and Arab pilots, also was a mystery which Russian aviation scientists were curious to fathom.

Following the Strecker affair, the story broke in Bei-

227

rut that two Soviet agents had paid one million French francs to a Lebanese Army pilot, with a promise of an additional two million francs, upon delivery of a Lebanese Mirage to Baku Airport in the capital of the U.S.S.R. Azerbedjan Republic. The Lebanese pilot, Mohammed Badawi, informed his Security Services.

When Lebanese military police, forced their way into the Soviet Embassy in Beirut to arrest the First Secretary, Alexander Komiakov, and his aide, Vladimir Vassiliev, they were met with resistance from Russian guards, and in the ensuing struggle, both U.S.S.R. Embassy officials were wounded.

Komiakov admitted to police that he tried to bribe Badawi to fly a Mirage to the Soviet Union, but the Lebanese authorities hushed up the affair to avoid disrupting diplomatic relations with Moscow. Komiakov and Vassiliev were diplomatically transferred to Moscow, where it was later learned that the former First Secretary of the Soviet Embassy in Beirut had held the rank of general in the Red Army Secret Service.

CHAPTER SIXTEEN

CHERBOURG

In May 1970, the spokesman of Israel's Defense Ministry surprised the world by publishing an official communique stating that Israeli engineers and technicians had succeeded in constructing a sea-to-sea missile of a range and power hitherto unknown for this kind of weapon both in the U.S.S.R. and in the West.

"Gabriel," as the Israelis called their missile, invoked the admiration of the military attaches and foreign correspondents accredited to Israel. Informed observers quickly drew two important conclusions from the public performance of the "Gabriel" missiles; first that these sea-to-sea missiles commanded an astonishing precision in firing at a long range, were equipped with an auto-guided electronic radar, and were designed to arm the famous Cherbourg gunboats, which had been built in France for Israel, but which, as a result of the embargo, had not been allowed to leave France; second, that Israel, owning a relatively important number of these gunboats equipped with "Gabriel" missiles, had found the proper tactical answer to the Komar and Ossa gunboats the U.S.S.R.

229

had delivered to Egypt—these were also equipped with sea-to-sea missiles, but of a quality inferior to the Israeli ones.

Thus it was only in May 1970, after Israel had revealed the secret of its "Gabriel" missiles, the project which had been initiated ten years earlier, that the world understood why Israel had risked a break in diplomatic relations with France at the time of the famous affair of the Cherbourg gunboats.

Israel had known, ever since its lightning 1967 victory against the Arabs, that it would eventually have to confront, on the ground, in the air, and on the sea, the most up-to-date and sophisticated weapons with which the Soviet Union supplied Arab armies, but that it also risked a direct confrontation with the ever more numerous units of the Red Army stationed in Egypt and Syria. The so-called "Cherbourg" gunboats, equipped with sea-to-sea missiles of Israeli make, constituted one of Israel's tactical responses to the presence of the Soviet fleet in the Mediterranean, just as the Phantoms and Skyhawks of American make were—and still are to this day—Israel's tactical response to the Mig 2's, and the Sam 2 and Sam 3 missiles the U.S.S.R. has installed in Egypt. It is hardly playing on words to recall in this context the famous French movie, "Les Parapluies de Cherbourg," and to maintain that for Israel in 1970, the Cherbourg gunboats are vitally important in providing it with a maritime "umbrella."

Since 1960 Israel's navy, the "step-child" of the armed forces of a country perpetually at war with its Arab neighbors, demanded from the General Staff and the Ministry of Defense, by any means and at any cost, fast gunboats equipped with guns and missiles, to enable it to measure up against the Egyptian Navy when such a need arose. Indeed, in 1960, Nasser had obtained from the Soviet Union thirty or so fast Komar gunboats, equipped with sea-to-sea missiles, with a range of forty kilometers.

It was in West Germany, which at the time, had not yet established diplomatic relations with Israel, that secret envoys of Israel's Ministry of Defense found naval equipment that seemed capable of countering the threat posed by the Soviet Komars: a fast gunboat, the "Jaguar," and a powerful Diesel engine, capable of propelling the craft at a speed of about seventy kilometers per hour, under battle conditions, and in a stormy sea. Thus, back in 1960, Israel ordered in Germany from a Hamburg ship-building firm twelve "Jaguar" gunboats, designed to meet the specific needs of Israel's Navy. The agreement, signed and ratified by the Bonn authorities, did not remain a secret.

The *New York Times* announced that Israel was secretly receiving supplies from Germany, with the blessing of Chancellor Adenauer, Mr. Ben Gurion's friend: helicopters, training planes, munitions, and fast gunboats were on their way from Germany to Israel. Then Nasser announced he would officially recognize East Germany and invited President Ulbricht to visit Cairo. West Germany established diplomatic relations with the State of Israel, but from then on refused to sell it arms. Even before it was built in Hamburg, the "Jaguar" was sacrificed to Bonn's political interests.

In 1965, soon after the establishment of diplomatic relations between Israel and the German Federal Republic, Tel Aviv's envoys selected the "Chantiers de Normandie," — whose Director General, Mr. Felix Amiot, was delighted to sign the Israeli contract—for the building of twelve missile-launching gunboats. These were developed from the German "Jaguars," but had been radically revised by the engineers and technicians of the Israeli Navy. The first gunboat, the "Mitvah" was launched on April 11, 1967, in the presence of the French local authorities, Israel's Ambassador to France, Mr. Walter Eytan, Admiral Mordechai Limon, head of Israel's purchasing Mission in Paris, Israel's Defense Ministry Delegation to Western Europe, and Admiral Shlomo Arell, Commander of the Israeli Navy. Among those attending the relatively discreet launching of the "Mitvah," was a high-ranking Israeli officer, then in training in Paris, General Haim Bar Lev, who by the end of the year would become Israel's Chief-of-Staff.

A number of Israeli journalists and press photographers had come especially from Tel Aviv for the occasion, and were invited by Mr. Amiot, but were forbidden to publish anything whatsoever about the gunboats.

France had allowed the building of the gunboats, which would later be equipped with weapons in Israel under license, but the authorities in Paris, wishing to spare Arab sensibilities, had requested Jerusalem to observe the greatest discretion on this subject.

That is why, in Cherbourg in 1967, one spoke of the "patrol boats" of the Israeli Navy, and never mentioned them by their real name, "Satil"—the Hebrew abbreviation for "missile launching boats."

When in April 1967 the first gunboat was anchored in Haifa's military port, the builders of the sea-to-sea missile "Gabriel" immediately undertook a first series of firing tests on the high sea.

On June 5, 1967, the Six Day War broke out. On the eve of the War, France declared the embargo, which tied up all military supplies earmarked for Israel. A few weeks after the war, the French Government modified its position, and discreetly applied a "selective" embargo; with the exception of the Mirages, grounded at the Dassault plant, most of the other Israeli orders reached their destination.

In the course of 1967 and 1968, Cherbourg delivered four additional gunboats, and stepped up the construction of the remaining ones. In December 1968, Israeli commandos carried out a lightning raid against Beirut Airport, from where the Popular Front for the Liberation of Palestine dispatched their assassins to carry out their attack against an Israeli Boeing in Athens.

On January 2, 1969, de Gaulle extended the embargo to apply to all military supplies destined to Israel.

The gunboats, in principle, would remain in Cherbourg. De Gaulle did not know—according to *Paris Match,* (January 1970)—that on December 31, 1968, three days after the Beirut raid, a sixth missile-launching craft had quietly left Cherbourg. The Israelis in Cher-

233

bourg heard about the embargo, which would soon be officially announced, and thereupon hastened to rescue this sixth boat.

According to the same source, they did better still; a seventh gunboat left Cherbourg forty-eight hours after the embargo was declared. The boat was designated by the code name "Acco," (the Hebrew name of Acre, North of Haifa); its paint was not yet dry, nor its engines run-in when, on Saturday January 4, 1969, late in the afternoon, this seventh boat left the Cherbourg navy yards. The crew was advised to tell the customs, in case they were stopped, that they were taking to sea for a series of trial tests. But, it was Saturday; and no questions were asked.

De Gaulle was furious when he learned about the departure of the seventh gunboat after the date on which the embargo became operative, and he demanded severe sanctions against the responsible French Navy officers. But the navy countered, documents in hand, that the embargo orders had only reached Cherbourg on January 6; and in any case, the responsible authorities in Cherbourg explained, the boats were not armed, so that it was not evident whether or not they were subjected to the embargo.

The controversy between the Elysée and the services of the French Navy lasted for quite some time. After January 1969, the five last gunboats under construction in Cherbourg were not anchored within the military yard but in a cilivian basin. The French Navy, rightly considering that these were foreign ships, did not want to bear responsibility for them to the French authorities. In due course, the boats would leave the port of Cherbourg all the more easily now that they were no longer under military guard.

On December 14, 1969, according to *Paris Match* the last of the gunboats, the "Hetz," (Arrow) was launched. The Israeli colony in Cherbourg—many naval officers and about fifty sailors, all of whom lived in a small hotel owned by the "Chantiers de Normandie"—prepared to sail off with the last five gunboats, which would join the seven already in Israel.

The running-in of the engines took place daily, and the sailors discreetly loaded the food supplies needed for the crossing from Cherbourg to Haifa via the Straits of Gibraltar. The Commander of the five gunboats, Colonel Ezra, a quiet, stocky man, whose smiling face was adorned by a big mustache, studied the more dangerous eastern pass to the high sea, and therefore less vigilantly watched than the western pass, generally used by ships leaving Cherbourg.

At the same time—exactly from the middle of November—another far more complicated game was being played in Paris in order to make it possible for the gunboats to leave, in spite of the embargo. On November 18, the Inter-ministerial Commission for the Study of Exports of War Supplies presided over by General Cazelles, former private secretary of War Minister Pierre Mesmer, decided to authorize the sale of the Israeli gunboats to a Company that claimed to be registered in Panama.

That day, the Commission, which in principle checks

on all sales of war supplies to foreign countries, studied the gunboat file and ascertained that they could not be considered war ships, and could perfectly well be sold to a Panama Company which intended to use them for underwater oil drilling; the boats were not armed, nor were they registered with any national navy.

Furthermore, the file contained a letter written by Admiral Mordechai Limon, Director of Israel's Purchasing Mission in Paris, whereby he declared in the name of his Government that these boats were no longer of any interest to Israel, and could therefore be sold to a third party. Finally, the file contained formal proof that there was a new buyer, who was prepared to pay cash for the craft. Mr. Felix Amiot, Director General of the "Chantiers de Normandie," had informed the Commission that a Panama Company, managed by a Norwegian businessman who was well known in maritime circles, Mr. Ole Martin Siem, wished to buy the boats which the Israelis no longer wanted. His company, the "Starboat Shipping and Oil Drilling Company," registered in Panama, dealt with oil drillings and had an office in Oslo. Mr. Siem came to Paris on October 13, where, after talking with Admiral Limon and asking him all kinds of technical questions about the gunboats, which he would like to use for drillings off the Alaska coast, met Mr. Amiot at his residence. Mr. Siem was prepared to pay Mr. Amiot fifty-five million Francs, the price of the five gunboats, and this would allow Mr. Amiot to return to the Israelis the twenty-two million Francs they had paid in deposit.

The C.I.E.E.M.G., did not know that Mr. Siem was

a close friend of Mr. Mila Brenner, an Israeli businessman who was director of the "Maritime Fruit Carriers
Ltd.," a Company which transported Israel's citrus fruit
all over the world. Neither did the Commission as yet
know that the "Starboat Company" had been especially
created to serve as a screen, that its shares were in the
hands of Mr. Brenner, and that the three Panama lawyers
of the firm "Arias Fabrega y Fabrega" who registered it
on November 5 as one of maritime companies of Panama
were also its directors.

The Inter-ministerial Commission harbored no suspicions in regard to the whole operation, set up so cleverly,
and it gave its agreement. A word for word copy of the
minutes of the Commission's secret meeting and of its
agreement was sent to the Prime Minister's office, where
it was filed in the archives. That same day—December
18—the official authorization to remit the five gunboats
to the "Starboat Company" reached Cherbourg. The moment had come for Colonel Ezra to get ready to sail. He
decided, with the agreement of Tel Aviv, that the gunboats would leave Cherbourg on December 24, that is on
Christmas Eve.

Hastily, signs reading "Starboat I, II," and so on, replaced the Hebrew names the gunboats had borne until
then—"Soufa," (Tempest), "Gaash," (Volcano), "He-
rev," (Sword), "Hanit," (Spear), and "Hetz," (Arrow).
A dressmaker in Equeudreville was asked to make Norwegian flags.

At the "Chantiers de Normandie," nothing was known
about the impending departure of the boats. Quite the

contrary, Mr. Amiot's engineers were convinced that weeks of testing and running-in were needed before the boats could safely sail to Norway, and from there to Alaska. Another proof that Colonel Ezra and his men were not planning to leave Cherbourg was that they had reserved places—eighty-eight in all—for Christmas parties in two of the city's restaurants.

On December 20, Mr. Amiot went to Cannes for the holidays, and the "Chantiers de Normandie" closed their doors for four days. Because of Christmas, the staffs of port services, and those of the police and customs were greatly reduced.

Everything had thus been arranged to facilitate the departure of the gunboats.

On December 24, around midnight, as people crowded in the churches to attend mass, Colonel Ezra, at the helm of the first gunboat, sailed away. The port watchmen, the policemen and the lookout men would only learn about the departure of the gunboats three days later, as they read their newspapers. As in so many other cases involving more or less clandestine shipments of arms and military equipment from France to Israel, it was a journalist who found out about it. Cherbourg's daily newspaper, *Le Phare de la Manche* never even mentioned the Israeli gunboats. Mr. Amiot, the director of the naval yards, had long before requested the newspaper's editor to abstain from any reportage concerning the twelve gunboats ordered by Israel, to avoid drawing the attention of Palestinian saboteurs, and of French circles hostile to Israel.

Cherbourg

But no such understanding existed between the "Chantiers de Normandie" and the important paper, *Ouest-France*. Its bureau chief in Cherbourg, Lemesle, learned on December 26, two days after their departure, that the gunboats had sailed on Christmas Eve. He called up his home office in Rennes, and notified them, "The gunboats sold to Norway have left." The international news agencies, A.P. and U.P. picked up the news which, via Paris and London, went round the world. Sensational headlines announced the news, first in London, and then around the world, and this was generally interpreted as a lifting by President Pompidou of the embargo clamped on by de Gaulle. Interviewed at 2 a.m., the next morning, the Defense Ministry spokesman in Paris told the journalists that nothing had changed and the embargo was still in force, and that the gunboats originally built for Israel had been sold to a Panama Company and were at that very moment sailing towards Norway.

But the international news agencies quickly found out that the five gunboats were sailing in the direction of Gibraltar.

It was now the turn of the President of the French Republic to get excited. On December 27, Pompidou received in Carjac a telephone call from the Secretary to the Presidency, informing him of the situation. Then it was the Minister of Foreign Affairs, Mr. Maurice Schumann, who called the President, upset to learn from the press that the embargo had been lifted. A few days later, as he went over the file, Mr. Schumann exclaimed, "They shouldn't get away with it!"

It was only on December 31 that a restricted Council of Ministers met with the President at the Elysée. It in‑cluded Premier Chaban Delmas, Michel Debré and Mau‑rice Schumann. It was decided to apply sanctions to the two generals of the Inter-ministerial Commission for hav‑ing been "imprudent."

At about this time, flocks of reconnaissance planes of all nationalities, French, Russian, Egyptian and Ameri‑can, were flying over the five gunboats which were being refueled on the high seas by an Israeli tanker which had rushed to meet them. Soon after, the gunboats entered Haifa's port, where about a hundred correspondents had been awaiting them for hours.

Few Frenchmen, and even fewer foreigners know that almost nothing concerning the affair of the Cherbourg gunboats escaped the notice of a handful of Frenchmen whose duty and mission it is to know everything. The French Intelligence officers (Renseignements Generaux). On December 20, four days before the gunboats sailed, Intelligence agents in Cherbourg informed their superiors in Paris that everything pointed to an imminent sailing of the gunboats. They had noted the existence of a direct radio link between the boats and Israel, had noticed the running-in of the engines, and found out that the sailors were loading supplies aboard, evidently preparing to de‑part on short notice.

Oddly, the report sent by the "Renseignements Gene‑raux" was filed away in some archives, and nobody, neither in the Ministry of the Interior nor at the Elysée ever mentioned it.

Cherbourg

The gunboats were still somewhere in the Mediterranean when another large scale operation, also carried out by Israeli soldiers, was taking place in another sea. This occurred on Friday December 26, in the Gulf of Suez, more exactly on the Egyptian Coast of the Gulf, at about two hundred kilometers south of the city of Suez. The goal of the operation, whose James Bond like details were only known a few days later, was to remove a Soviet radar in perfect operating order, together with all its installations and bring it over to Israel for the purpose of tactical studies. An Israeli commando group carried out the operation.

The merit of the kidnapping can be attributed to Israel's Chief-of-Staff, General Haim Bar Lev. Israel's pilots had pounded Egyptian positions along the Gulf of Suez time and time again in December 1969, and were aware that a radar station, somewhere near Ras Gareb, two hundred kilometers south of Suez, was causing them trouble. It seemed to be a radar of the latest type, since it could intercept Israeli planes flying at a very low altitude. The Commander of Israel's Air Force supplied the necessary intelligence data to the Chief-of-Staff.

On December 26, General Bar Lev was somewhere in Sinai with the Commando Unit selected to carry out the operation. "The whole of Israel's army is behind you, ready to intervene if necessary," the General told the soldiers before they left. They crossed the Gulf without hindrance and after nightfall came near the hill, a few kilometers from the coast, where the radar was located. Great was the surprise of the five Egyptian soldiers in charge of the radar when they understood that they were encircled by Israelis. The Soviet radar in question was of the P. 12 type, one almost unknown in the West, which can detect planes flying at a low altitude; it was linked to a ground-to-air Sam 2 missile base, installed a few kilometers away. The radar, mounted on two Soviet trucks of the "Zil" type, weighed seven tons; it was made up of two units, one weighing three tons, the other four.

Throughout the night, the Israeli technicians who had come with the commandos were at work, carefully taking apart the two units of the radar. It was only with the first glimmer of dawn that their job was completed. The radar parts were fixed to two helicopters which had flown from Sinai, and which were to take them back to Israel. On the way back, one of the helicopters ran into serious mechanical difficulties and its pilot received the order to discharge his load into the Dead Sea. But the pilot refused and managed to land in Israel with his four ton load.

The Chief-of-Staff, who had waited all night long for the return of the Commando Unit, declared, "What you have accomplished is worthy of a James Bond movie." His words were quoted by the press, which nevertheless said nothing about the radar, only mentioning that a Commando Unit had brought several prisoners back from Egypt. No one in Israel as yet understood the meaning of General Bar Lev's unusual praise to this Commando Unit; for political reasons the Israeli Government had decided not to release any information about this sensational kidnapping. A high-ranking officer had already called military correspondents to give them the pictures of the radar and relate the details of the operation. But the world-wide reaction which had followed upon the news of the "kidnapping" of the Cherbourg gunboats caused the Ministers in Jerusalem to change their minds.

"We are already accused of having behaved as pirates in France. The radar business, if published now, would only confirm the negative image of Israel abroad," a Minister who carried great weight said in Jerusalem, according to foreign sources.

As the news was whispered from mouth to ear, almost everybody knew about the radar before the night of December 31, 1969. But the story of the remarkable feat hit the headlines of the world press only after the *Daily Express* in London published the main features of the story. The story has often been mentioned in the Israeli press, but always using the *Daily Express* as source of reference.

Officially, and probably for quite some time, the five Cherbourg gunboats are still owned by the "Starboat Company" of Panama, and the Soviet radar was never lifted from the Gulf of Suez.